T0065648

Pandolfini's
E N D G A M E
Course

by

B R U C E   P A N D O L F I N I

A FIRESIDE BOOK
Published by Simon & Schuster
New York London Toronto Sydney

ACKNOWLEDGMENTS

I would like to thank Bruce Alberston, Doug Bellizzi, Deborah Bergman, Jennifer Bruer, Carol Ann Caronia, Kris Catalano, Bonni Leon, Idelle Pandolfini, Bruce Steinitz, Larry Tamarkin, George Wen, and Laura Yorke for their time and valuable work. They made the whole thing possible.

For Rosie and Joe, and Margie and Fred

FIRESIDE
Rockefeller Center
1230 Avenue of the Americas
New York, New York 10020

Published by the Simon & Schuster Trade Division

FIRESIDE and colophon are registered trademarks
of Simon & Schuster Inc.

Manufactured in the United States of America

20 19

Library of Congress Cataloging in Publication Data

Pandolfini, Bruce.
   Pandolfini's endgame course / by Bruce Pandolfini.
      p. cm.
   "A Fireside book."
   Includes index.
   1. Chess—End games. I. Title. II. Title: Endgame course.
GV1450.7.P45 1988
794.1'24—dc19   88-17465
                                                              CIP

ISBN-13: 978-0-671-65688-1
ISBN-10:   0-671-65688-0

CONTENTS

5

$$\boxed{II}$$

THE PAWNS IN ACTION

PIECES AND PAWNS IN ACTION

Introduction

I became a chess teacher in 1972, during the dazzling Bobby Fischer/Boris Spassky World Chess Championship that inspired the world to learn chess. Suddenly, I had many students and needed ideas and examples for lessons. I turned to the literature of the royal game for source material. Although I discovered many volumes on the opening and middlegame, I quickly realized that endgame books were few and far between.

This wasn't the only problem. Existing books on chess endings were of two unsatisfactory types. Either they were too analytic and technical or too vague and general. There was a compelling need to combine the best features of both types into a single instructional format.

So on my own I started to collect insightful endgame positions, explaining in both words and chess variations the concepts I judged to be the most helpful to my students. Numerous examples were organized, classified, and arranged into complete courses. My goal was to create an inventory of positions that would benefit any chessplayer who studied them. Eventually, I settled upon a nucleus of 200 problems that became the basic course in the endgame. With some additions and modifications, that compendium is what I present here.

The examples in *Pandolfini's Endgame Course* are arranged in three major sections. Part One, called Pieces in Action, deals with basic mates and confrontations mainly between unlike pieces. In Part Two The Pawns in Action, the principles of pawn endings are illustrated, including the key concepts of opposition, square of the pawn, and critical squares. Pieces and Pawns in Action constitutes Part Three, which displays how various pieces grapple with advancing passed pawns.

Pandolfini's Endgame Course has a simple, easy-to-use format. Each page has a large, clear diagram, introduced with a directive cue (such as "White moves and wins"), and characterized by a descriptive term or phrase (such as "Cut-Off"). An explanatory passage providing the essential ideas, moves, and alternate lines of play follows the cue. The main variation appears in boldface type. Each variation concludes in mate, overwhelming advantage, stalemate, or unambiguous draw.

Within each chapter, every attempt has been made to organize the problems in a gradual progression from simple to complex, but occasionally the course must veer from this formula for instructive purposes. Though no complicated "textbook" positions have been included, the book nevertheless is concerned with the building blocks on which they are based. So, while intricate discussions of corresponding square theory have been omitted, for example, the theoretical groundwork of square theory has been laid down in the problems on triangulation.

Some endgame books contain thousands of positions but are impenetrable and therefore useless to the average chessplayer. Every one of my 239 positions can be understood, even by able beginners. And some of these positions—such as those on the Queen and Rook mate—are discussed in no other endgame book and, perhaps, in no other chess book.

I advise reading *Pandolfini's Endgame Course* from start to finish. That's how I usually present the examples to my students, regardless of their level of play. But you might prefer reading specific sections first. Perhaps there's a concept you'd like to understand, or a position you need to check. Whatever your reasons for turning to my course, should it translate to more victories in the endgame, and more fun in the end.

About Algebraic Notation

The best way to read this book is while sitting at a chessboard on the White side, with the pieces starting on the same squares as those in the examples you're considering. Much of the material can be understood without playing out the moves, by either reading the descriptive comments or examining the helpful diagrams accompanying the text. But you will derive greater benefit if you learn the simplified algebraic notation offered here. The system works as follows:

- The board is regarded as an eight-by-eight graph with sixty-four squares in all.
- The *files* (the rows of squares going up the board) are lettered *a* through *h*, beginning from White's left.
- The *ranks* (the rows of squares going across the board) are numbered 1 through 8, beginning from White's nearest row.

You can therefore identify any square by combining a letter and a number, with the letter written first (see diagram A). For example, the square on which White's King stands in the original position is "e1," while the original square for Black's King is "e8." All squares are always named from White's point of view.

Symbols You Should Know

K	King
Q	Queen
R	Rook
B	Bishop
N	Knight

Pawns are not symbolized when recording moves. But if referred to in discussions, they are named by the letter of the file occupied: for example, the pawn on the b-file is the "b-pawn." If a pawn makes a capture, one merely indicates the file the capturing pawn starts on. This, if a White pawn on b2 captures a Black pawn, Knight, Bishop, Rook, or Queen on a3, it is written as **bxa3.** When indicating a capture, name the square captured, not the enemy unit.

Here are some more symbols you should know:

×	captures
+	check
0-0	castles Kingside
0-0-0	castles Queenside
!	good move

!!	very good move
?	questionable move
??	blunder
?!	risky move but worth considering
!?	probably a good move but unclear
1.	White's first move
1. . . .	Black's first move (when appearing independently of White's)
(1–0)	White wins
(0–1)	Black wins

And a few other symbols to know:

RP	Rook-pawn
NP	Knight-pawn
BP	Bishop-pawn
CP	Center-pawn

Reading the Line Score of a Game

Consider diagram B. White could mate in three moves, and it could be written this way:

1. Nc7 +   Kb8   2. Na6 +   Ka8   3. Bc6   mate

The same moves could be written in chart form, with White's moves on the left and Black's corresponding moves on the right:

1. Nc7 +   Kb8
2. Na6 +   Ka8
3. Bc6   mate

In both cases:

1. **Nc7+** means that White's first move is Knight to c7, giving check.
   Kb8 means that Black's first move is King to b8.
2. **Na6+** means that White's second move is Knight to a6 check.
   Ka8 means that Black's second move is King to a8.
3. **Bc6 mate** means that White's third move is Bishop to c6 mate.

Note that when the moves appear on a line across the page, the number of the move is written only once, just before White's play. In this book, the actual moves are given in boldface type. The analyzed alternatives appear in regular type.

P A R T
ONE

Pieces in Action

The basis of all chess knowledge is an understanding of the powers of the pieces—their individual and collective potentials.

In Part One, the board is unencumbered by any pawns, and the pieces hold full sway. The first two chapters demonstrate the minimum level of force required to mate the lone king. Commonly called the Basic or Elementary Mates, they vary in difficulty.

Mates with the heavy (or major) pieces are by far the easiest to accomplish and require only minimal assistance from the King. By contrast, mates with the light (or minor) pieces demand the King's full cooperation and are rather more intricate to execute, since each piece must stretch itself to the limit.

In Chapters 3 and 4, we examine six of the most common endings, in which White and Black pieces are in conflict with each other. The practical is emphasized over the theoretical. For example, abstract theory pronounces that the Rook and minor-piece endings of Chapter 4 usually end in a draw. But by featuring the exceptions, where one side actually wins, we can understand more fully why more typical positions tend to end in a draw.

Finally, we must mention the fifty-move rule. It states that "the game is drawn when a player having the move demonstrates that at least fifty consecutive moves have been played by each side without capture of any piece or the movement of any pawn." This rule has a vital bearing on endings in Part One, in which there are no pawns and trades must be avoided if enough material is to be left on the board to force mate. If the stronger side plays inaccurately, fifty moves might pass and the defender could claim a draw.

1

Elementary Checkmates: Heavy Pieces

ENDGAME 1

W: Ke1, Qd1, Rf4 B: Ke5
White moves and wins

Queen and Rook Roll

This is the simplest, fastest, most basic checkmate of all. From any initial arrangement of pieces, White should force mate in no more than five to six moves. The Queen and Rook alternatively heel each other up a staircase of supportive checks known as "the roll." Mate comes in four moves.

1. Qd4 +   Ke6
2. Rf6 +   Ke7 +
3. Qd6 +   Ke8
4. Rf8   mate

(1–0)

ENDGAME 2

W: Ke1, Qa3, Rb4 B: Ke5
White moves and wins

Rolling Barrier

In this more typical Queen and Rook roll, the two major pieces stand on adjacent files and give alternate checks to drive Black's King to the board's edge. The Rook's barrier is upheld against diagonal attack by the Queen. Finally, the major pieces guard consecutive outside rows, preventing escape and mating.

1.	Qa5+	Kd6
2.	Rb6+	Kc7
3.	Qa7+	Kc8
4.	Rb8	mate

(1–0)

ENDGAME 3

W: Kf1, Rh2, Rh1 B: Kg8
White moves and wins

Rook Barrier

Two Rooks mate much the same way as Queen and Rook, but not as quickly, since additional temporizing moves are required to ward off diagonal counterattacks. White has two ways to mate in three moves in the diagram: (A) by cutting off the King on the f-file and rolling the Rooks on the files rightward; and (B) by occupying the 7th rank on the h-file, shifting the other Rook to the adjacent g-file, gaining a tempo on Black's King, and mating up the board on the 8th rank. In both ways, the Rooks will impede each other if they perform on the same line. Instead they shift to adjacent rows, thereby dominating blocks of sixteen squares.

A			B	
1. Rf2	Kg7		1. Rh7	Kf8
2. Rg1+	Kh6		2. Rg1	Ke8
3. Rh2	mate		3. Rg8	mate
(1–0)			(1–0)	

ENDGAME 4

W: Kd5, Qd7 B: Ka8
White moves and wins

Closing In

A King and Queen mate a lone King on an outside row by checking along the edge—a back row mate—or by the Queen's checking up close, protected by its King—a support mate. The latter, as in the diagram, is the "one, two, three formula": the losing King is trapped on an outside row (1); the Queen occupies the row adjacent to the edge (2); and the White King, on a square in the next row (3), defends the Queen.

1. Kc6   Kb8
2. Qb7   mate
     (1–0)

ENDGAME 5

Backing Off

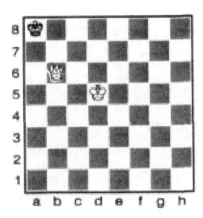

To push the King to the edge, the Queen gradually snips off the King's available squares, move by move, closing in at a "Knight's jump away." Overly rigid execution of this procedure, however, stalemates Black's King in the corner—Black to move is already stalemated. White to play wins by retreating the Queen one square along the barrier (the b-file), giving Black breathing room against stalemate. White's King then moves in to support mate.

1. Qb5   Ka7
2. Kc6   Ka8
3. Qb7 mate
(1–0)

ENDGAME **6**

Cut-Off

Here the pieces are positioned in a one, two, three formula, as in Endgame 4. But in this version White's King has to chase Black's before getting close enough to support mate. This *could* take a whopping five moves, as in 1. Kf6 Kh4 2. Kf5 Kh3 3. Kf4 Kh2 4. Kf3 Kh1 5. Qg2 mate. The more efficient choice is to execute a timely cut-off with the Queen, forcing Black's King back the other way and saving three moves. On his final move, White could also mate by 2. **Qh4**.

1. **Qg3   Kh6**
2. **Qg6 mate**
(1–0)

ENDGAME 7

W: Kc5, Qh1 B: Ke8
White moves and wins

Erecting the Barrier

To keep Black's King caged on the edge, White's Queen is posted on the very next line. The placement establishes a cordon against escape. Next, White's King claims the row behind its consort's, eventually overwhelming its counterpart for a back-row mate or supporting a close-up Queen check. Again, Black's King occupies row 1, White's Queen row 2, and White's King row 3.

A	
1. Qh7	Kf8
2. Kd6	Ke8
3. Qe7	mate
(1–0)	

B	
1. Qh7	Kd8
2. Kd6	Kc8
3. Qc7	mate
(1–0)	

ENDGAME **8**

Waiting-Move Mate

King and Rook against King can't end in a support mate (don't even try to set one up). Go for a back-row mate instead, the Rook checking and White's King guarding the possible escape squares. White's King must stand directly opposite Black's on the same rank or file. (The exception: If Black's King is in the corner, White's King need only be on the adjacent line.) However, a word of warning—if White should move his King immediately into line (1. Kf6), Black just slips away (1. . . . Ke8) and White must start all over again. White instead should move to get Black to align with White's King. This is done through a tempo move or waiting move. The Rook slides one square along the 7th rank, changing nothing essential in the position, but turning the move over to Black.

1.	Rb7	Kg8
2.	Kf6	Kh8
3.	Kg6	Kg8
4.	Rb8	mate

(1–0)

ENDGAME 9

W: Ke6, Rd5 B: Kf8
White moves and wins

The "Cut-Off" Mate

A conscientious Rook can work wonders. The right tempo or cut-off can reduce Black's King to an automaton, with no options. Instead of taking the 7th rank here (1. Rd7), White gains more by cordoning off the g-file, forcing Black to oppose White's King. A back-rank mate in two moves can thus be realized. In the final position, the three pieces form a right triangle, with Black's King at the base.

1. **Rg5**   Ke8
2. **Rg8**   mate
(1–0)

ENDGAME **10**

W: Ke6, Re2 B: Ke8
White moves and wins

The Any-Rook Move Mate

Giving a discovered check is irresistible, but forget it here. Instead, work the Rook and finally force a back-row, right-triangle mate. The solution is quite astonishing, for White mates in three moves, starting with any Rook move—that's right, with any of eleven Rook moves available! But note that on the second play, the Rook must occupy a cut-off file, forcing Black's King to line up with White's. As variations A and B demonstrate, there is no significant difference if White moves his Rook initially along the file or the rank. In either case, Black's King winds up mated at e8.

A		B	
1. **Re5**	**Kd8**	1. **Ra2**	**Kf8**
2. **Rc5**	**Ke8**	2. **Rg2**	**Ke8**
3. **Rc8**	**mate**	3. **Rg8**	**mate**
(1–0)		(1–0)	

ENDGAME **11**

W: Kf5, Re5 B: Kg7
White moves and wins

Closing the Net

Roping off could be better than giving a Rook check. Players naturally hanker to cage Black's King with 1. Re6, when barriers are then maintained on the e-file and 6th rank. More comes, however, with a Rook check at e7, shaping the three pieces into a triangle. With this incursion, precise Rook work trounces Black quickly. After 1. **Re7+** Kh6 2. Rf7 Kh5, White mates by 3. Rh7. White's second move, a tempo waster, can be taken by the Rook on any square between f7 and a7. The struggle goes on with the sidling 1. . . . **Kf8**, but ultimately fails to the same tempo-reversing mechanism: 2. Kf6 Kg8 3. Kg6 (or 3. Re8+ Kh7 4. Rf8 Kh6 5. Rh8 mate) **Kf8** 4. Re6 (the tempo move that can happen anywhere between e6 and e1) 4. . . . **Kg8** 5. **Re8 mate.**

1.	Re7+	Kf8
2.	Kf6	Kg8
3.	Kg6	Kf8
4.	Re6	Kg8
5.	Re8	mate

(1–0)

2

Elementary Checkmates: Minor Pieces

ENDGAME 12

W: Kc7, Bb4, Bb3 B: Ka6
White moves and wins

The Bishop Roll

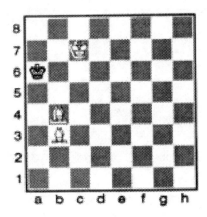

Even as Rooks can occupy adjacent rows and drive the King to the edge by alternate checks, so can bishops, more or less. Yes, they need help from their King, whereas Rooks do not. And true, it takes a little longer, but nevertheless mate is forced in the corner.

1. Bc4+   Ka7
2. Bc5+   Ka8
3. Bd5   mate
(1–0)

ENDGAME **13**

Positioning the King

Before dealing mate, White must prevent Black's escape by 1. **Kb6.** After 1. . . . **Ka8,** White declines seizure of the adjacent leftward diagonal (2. Be5), which would result in stalemate. The dark-square Bishop may occupy the b8-h2 diagonal only after black has played his King to b8. A waiting move shifts the tempo to Black. This means shifting either Bishop to safe squares along diagonals each already controls (the c8-h3 diagonal for the light-square Bishop, and the d8-h4 diagonal for its dark-square partner). With 1. **Kb6 Ka8,** White temporizes 2. **Be7,** and after 2 . . . . **Kb8,** the Bishops slide into mating mode 3. **Bd6 + Ka8** 4. **Bd5 mate.**

1.	Kb6	Ka8
2.	Be7	Kb8
3.	Bd6 +	Ka8
4.	Bd5	mate

(1–0)

ENDGAME 14

	W: Kc6, Bf7, Bg7 **B**: Kb8
	White moves and wins

Closing the Door

If White tries 1. Kb6, as in the previous example, Black swings back to the center 1. ... Kc8, and White's Bishops cannot guard both holes at d7 and d8 in one move. And White's King and Bishops are separated and fall short of working harmoniously. A purposeful Bishop move is what's required here, enabling White to tighten the noose without losing time. Either Bishop can have the honor.

	A			**B**	
1.	Bd4	Kc8	1.	Bc4	Kc8
2.	Bf6	Kb8	2.	Bf6	Kb8
3.	Kb6	Kc8	3.	Kb6	Kc8
4.	Be6+	Kb8	4.	Be6+	Kb8
5.	Be5+	Ka8	5.	Be5+	Ka8
6.	Bd5	mate	6.	Bd5	mate
	(1–0)			(1–0)	

ENDGAME **15**

W: Kc6, Bd5, Be5 B: Kf8
White moves and wins

Taking Away Squares

White's pieces are a trigger-fine army, with each unit ready for mayhem. To confine Black's King to an outside row, White's Bishops tandem in a double-vee barrier, while the King guards potential escape squares. Once the enemy King is surrounded, adjacent diagonals can be methodically controlled, one after the other, until the monarch is cornered. Two sample variations of different length are offered. Variation A concludes after 7. **Kb6**, as in Endgame 13; variation B terminates after 5. **Bd4**, as in Endgame 14.

	A		**B**	
1.	Kd6	Ke8	1. Kd6	Ke8
2.	Bg7	Kd8	2. Bg7	Kd8
3.	Bf7	Kc8	3. Bf7	Kc8
4.	Kc6	Kd8	4. Kc6	Kb8
5.	Bf6 +	Kc8	5. Bd4 +	
6.	Be6 +	Kb8	(1–0)	
7.	Kb6			
	(1–0)			

ENDGAME **16**

W: Kf7, Bf8, Ng4 B: Kh8
White moves and wins

Mate in Two

A Bishop-Knight mate can be forced only in a corner guarded by the Bishop. The two minor pieces share responsibilities. If the Bishop moves on dark squares, the Knight should guard light squares. Here the Bishop flushes out the King and the Knight confers the *coup de grace*.

1. **Bb7+** Kh7
2. **Nf6** mate
(1–0)

ENDGAME **17**

W: Kf7, Bg5, Ne5 B: Kh8
White moves and wins

Mate in Three

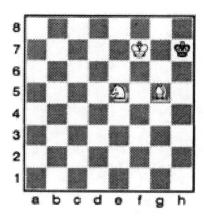

In this scenario, the Knight sets up the death blow, and the Bishop deals it. The three pieces line up chorus-line fashion in the end, though the Bishop could be equally ruthless on b2, c3, d4, or e5. Meanwhile, the light squares are held by the tandem King and Knight.

1. Ng6 +   Kh7
2. Nf8 +   Kh8
3. Bf6   mate

(1–0)

ENDGAME 18

W: Kg6, Bb4, Ng7 B: Kg8
White moves and wins

Mate in Four

This position comes from inching Black's King step by step from a8 to h8. On the previous move, the Bishop checked the King at f8, forcing it to g8. The next square White must control is g8, by mobilizing the Knight. But the Knight must not block the Bishop's diagonal. Also, White must avoid giving stalemate, which would happen if he attacked g8 while Black's King was still on h8. Everything clicks, thanks to a temporizing Bishop shift along the a3-e7 diagonal.

1.	Nf5	Kh8
2.	Be7	Kg8
3.	Nh6 +	Kh8
4.	Bf6	mate

(1–0)

ENDGAME 19

W: Ke8, Bf8, Ne5 **B:** Kg8
White moves and wins

Another Mate in Four

Black's King is about to depart g8, leaving the way open for White's King to enter f7. This means that the Knight can relinquish its coverage of g6 and reposition to control h7. Starting from e5, the Knight has three equally good ways to begin deployment: **1. Nd7**, **1. Nf3**, and **1. Ng4**.

	A	
1.	Nd7	Kh7
2.	Kf7	Kh8
3.	Bg7 +	Kh7
4.	Nf8	mate
	(1–0)	

	B	
1.	Nd7	Kh8
2.	Kf7	Kh7
3.	Nf6 +	Kh8
4.	Bg7	mate
	(1–0)	

ENDGAME **20**

W: Ke6, Bg5, Ne7 B: Kh7
White moves and wins

A Third Mate in Four

On the back row, Black's King has a mere two squares—g8 and h8—to play with, but there's also refuge at g7. White sniffs the danger and moves in with his own King.

1.	Kf7	Kh8
2.	Ng6+	Kg8
3.	Nf8+	Kh8
4.	Bf6	mate

(1–0)

ENDGAME 21

W: Kd6, Bg5, Ne5 B: Ke8
White moves and wins

The Lock

Even without the presence of White's ·King, Black's King is trapped in a Bishop-Knight net. Only six unguarded squares lie within the cordon: e8, f8, g8, g7, h8, and h7. White's plan is so simple: the King is maneuvered from the Queenside, usurping e8 and f8, until the Bishop can transfer safely to the f8-h6 diagonal. Mate follows, as in earlier endgames.

1.	Kc7	Kf8
2.	Kd7	Kg7
3.	Ke7	Kg8
4.	Bh6	Kh7
5.	Bf8	Kg8
6.	Ng4	Kh7
7.	Kf7	Kh8
8.	Bg7 +	Kh7
9.	Nf6	mate

(1–0)

ENDGAME 22

W: Kd6, Be3, Ne7 **B:** Kf7
White moves and wins

Transition to the Lock

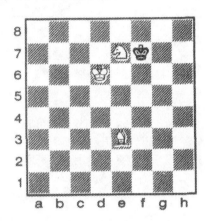

To seal the door, White's Knight must be at e5 and his Bishop at g5. The King then ankles in from the flank. The antique move here used to be 1. Bd4, expropriating the a1-h8 diagonal. But stronger is 1. **Bg5**, followed by the Knight to e5, creating a lock. Depending on Black's defense, he is mated either at h7 by the Knight or at h8 by the Bishop. After three moves, the position transforms into Endgame 21. Mate is forced in nine moves.

1.	Bg5	Ke8	7. Bh6	Kh7
2.	Ng6	Kf7	8. Bf8	Kg8
3.	Ne5 +	Ke8	9. Ng4	Kh7
4.	Kc7	Kf8	10. Kf7	Kh8
5.	Kd7	Kg7	11. Bg7 +	Kh7
6.	Ke7	Kg8	12. Nf6	mate

(1–0)

ENDGAME **23**

The King Shift

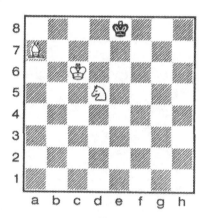

If Black's King starts in a corner of opposite color to the Bishop, it must be systematically driven across the board to a corner of the same color. Thus if in a light corner, the King must be forced to a dark one, if that's the color traveled by the Bishop. All three pieces meanwhile must integrate their unique powers to form a united force. Here, White's King occupies d6 to support the Knight's reaching e7, where it seals off c8 and guards potential escape squares at f5 and g6. The Bishop then skims to e3, controlling g5 and leading to the previous net. In the final position, after 1. **Kd6 Kf7** 2. **Ne7 Kf6** 3. **Be3 Kf7** 4. **Bg5**, White quickly reaches the winning lock.

1.	**Kd6**	Kf7		9.	**Ke7**	Kg8
2.	**Ne7**	Kf6		10.	**Bh6**	Kh7
3.	**Be3**	Kf7		11.	**Bf8**	Kg8
4.	**Bg5**	Ke8		12.	**Ng4**	Kh7
5.	**Ng6**	Kf7		13.	**Kf7**	Kh8
6.	**Ne5 +**	Ke8		14.	**Bg7 +**	Kh7
7.	**Kc7**	Kf8		15.	**Nf6**	mate
8.	**Kd7**	Kg7			(1–0)	

ENDGAME 24

W: Kc6, Be3, Nd5 B: Ka8
White moves and wins

The Drive

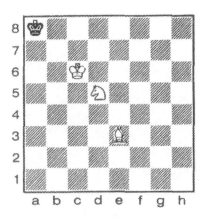

When Black's King is entrenched in the "wrong" corner of the board (a corner that is not accessible to White's Bishop), it can be driven to either opposite corner (here, a1 or h8). It all begins with a Knight check: 1. Nc7+ to force the King to h8, or 1. Nb6+ for a parallel attack toward a1. For consistency with previous endgames, the h8-drive is shown, but a mirror-image attack ending on a1 works just as well. Whatever the approach, it is accomplished step by step, controlling in sequence one square after the other along the outside row. The Knight hits the light squares, the Bishop attacks the dark squares, and the King performs the multiple functions, protecting the Knight while confining the enemy King. Tempo moves, as required, are left to the Bishop, a straight-line piece, which acts at a distance. After 1. Nc7+ Kb8 2. Bb6 (tempo) Kc8 3. Ba7 Kd8 4. Nd5 Ke8, White wins, as in the previous endgame.

1.	Nc7+	Kb8
2.	Bb6	Kc8
3.	Ba7	Kd8
4.	Nd5	Ke8
5.	Kd6	Kf7
6.	Ne7	Kf6
7.	Be3	Kf7
8.	Bg5	Ke8
9.	Ng6	Kf7
10.	Ne5+	Ke8
11.	Kc7	Kf8
12.	Kd7	Kg7
13.	Ke7	Kg8
14.	Bh6	Kh7
15.	Bf8	Kg8
16.	Ng4	Kh7
17.	Kf7	Kh8
18.	Bg7+	Kh7
19.	Nf6	mate

(1–0)

3

Heavy Pieces in Combat

ENDGAME 25

W: Kb3, Qd1 **B:** Kh1, Qg1, Qh2
White moves and draws

Perpetual Check

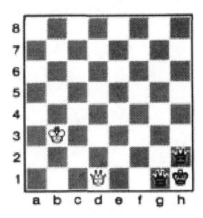

Generally, if you promote a pawn into an extra Queen, you win easily. But sometimes, if enemy pieces have harried your King, or if you have had plain bad luck, your pieces might simply huddle together ineffectually, unable to exploit their advantage. Here, the White Queen demonstrates its ability to check unbrokenly, resulting in a draw by threefold repetition of position.

1. Qf3 +   Qgg2
2. Qd1 +   Qhg1
3. Qh5 +   Q2h2
4. Qf3 +   Qgg2
5. Qd1 +   Qhg1
6. Qf3 +
        Draw

ENDGAME **26**

Forced Mate

W: Kb4, Qd2 **B:** Kb1, Qa1
White moves and wins

From the sublime to the ridiculous. Your opponent Queens a pawn before you do. Imagine the relief when you manage to equalize the game and Queen one yourself. As a draw appears certain, your opponent moves up his King and threatens mate. You are shocked when you realize that your pieces, stumbling over each other, cannot organize a defense. Such could be the case when your pawn-made Queen occupies a Rook's file. After White's King Intrudes at b3, Black succumbs to the multiple threats of Qc2, Qd1, or Qe1.

1. Kb3   Qc3 +
2. Kxc3   Ka1
3. Qb2   mate
(1–0)

ENDGAME 27

W: Kd6, Qe8 B: Kf6, Qg1
White moves and wins

The X-Ray Attack

Pawns racing to make new Queens is an exciting show. The first new Queen gets to give the first check, perhaps pitching a whole new ball game. Maybe Black can defend, or maybe White can pick off Black's princess. The tactic usually involves a skewer, or x-ray attack. Black's King moves out of check and exposes his Queen to capture. If Black's pieces are not yet on the same rank, file, or diagonal, White might force the opposing King into a losing skewer-lineup with a setup check. Black, here, after moving his King to safety, loses his Queen for nothing.

1. Qf8+   Kg6
2. Qg8+   Kf5
3. Qxg1
       (1–0)

ENDGAME **28**

Stalemate Sacrifice

Given a fair starting position of King and Queen vs. King and Rook, in which there are no immediate tactics, the stronger side can force a win. But not all positions are devoid of stratagems. For example, when the attacking pieces haphazardly encroach upon the defending monarch's up-against-the-wall situation, it is often possible to sacrifice the Rook to arrive at stalemate.

1. **Rh3 +**   **Kxh3**
   Stalemate

ENDGAME 29

W: Kf1, Rg2 B: Kh3, Qe3
White moves and draws

Perpetual Attack

You might have been supercareful to avoid a stalemate shot, then one suddenly rears. Black was canny enough to block entry with his King at f3, thus avoiding the draw of Endgame 28. But widening the field and invading at h3 doesn't help, for White retains his stalemate stealth. The Rook simply checks at h2, and its capture is stalemate. Otherwise, the Rook checks along the files repeatedly, and Black's King can't find shelter. If it ever moves to f3, White sacrifices his Rook at g3 for stalemate; and if Black's King instead seeks haven behind the Queen on the e-file, White's Rook pins the Queen to the King. Black cannot feasibly escape the checks, so the game is a draw.

1. **Rh2 +**
Draw

ENDGAME 30

W: Kf6, Qe8 B: Kh7, Rg7
White moves and wins

Philidor's Position

This position was originally analyzed by the great French master Francois-Andres Danican Philidor (1726–95). Black to move gets mated or loses his Rook in no more than four moves. For example: (A) 1. . . .Kh6   2. Qf8; (B) 1. . . .Rg8   2. Qh5 mate; (C) 1. . . .Rg1   2. Qe4+ Kg8   3. Qa8+ Kh7   4. Qa7+. Whatever else Black tries leads to a similarly dismal result. But it's not Black's turn! White must somehow recreate the same position with Black to move. The trick is to triangulate the Queen between e8, e4, and a8, so that White achieves the same position while losing a tempo. Three crisp moves do it.

1. Qe4 +   Kg8
2. Qa8 +   Kh7
3. Qe8
        (1–0)

ENDGAME **31**

W: Kd6, Qb5 **B:** Kc8, Ra7
White moves and wins

From Edge to Edge

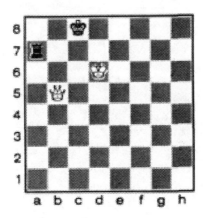

Black's pieces are awry. Neither of his pieces supports the other. Black's Rook is powerless to check, and his King is vulnerable to direct attack. The proper sequence of checks spreads chaos, resulting in catatonia for the losing side. Gradually, White's Queen hounds Black's King from the 8th rank to the a-file: 1. **Qe8+ Kb7** 2. **Qd7+ Kb8** 3. **Qd8+ Kb7** 4. **Qc7+ Ka6** (if Black tries 4. . . .Ka8, he's mated at once by 5. Qc8) 5. **Qc6+ Ka5**. White's King moves in to mop up with 6. **Kc5**, after which Black is mated in at most three moves, even if he delays with a Rook sacrifice: (A) 6. . . .Rb7 7. Qxb7 Ka4 8. Qb4 mate; or (B) 6. . . .Rc7 7. Qxc7+ Ka4 8. Qg3 Ka5 9. Qa3 mate.

1. Qe8 +	Kb7	6. Kc5	Rc7
2. Qd7 +	Kb8	7. Qxc7 +	Ka4
3. Qd8 +	Kb7	8. Qg3	Ka5
4. Qc7 +	Ka6	9. Qa3	mate
5. Qc6 +	Ka5		(1–0)

ENDGAME **32**

W: Ke6, Qc5 B: Kd8, Rd7
White moves and wins

Double-Threat Queen

It's easy to go wrong and waste time, even draw the game. Checks lead nowhere, and the invasion 1. Qc6 is met by 1. . . .Re7+, when White must sidestep 2. Kd6 Re6+ 3. Kxe6 stalemate. You can find the right move by pretending Black's Rook doesn't exist. Pretend too that you have carte blanche, that you can deposit your Queen on any square, even if the Queen cannot actually move there in the given position. Imagining thus helps you visualize your proper goals. If you continue the fantasy, without the Rook it would be mate if White's Queen could occupy d7 or b8. But really, with the Rook on the board, one Queen move attacks both points.

1.	**Qb5**	**Re7+**
2.	**Kd6**	**Rc7**
3.	**Qb6**	**Ke8**
4.	**Qxc7**	**Kf8**
5.	**Qh7**	**Ke8**
6.	**Qe7**	**mate**

(1–0)

ENDGAME **33**

W: Ke6, Qc3 B: Kd8, Rd1
White moves and wins

Dual Methods

You could win two ways in this position. Give a series of checks
to pick off the Rook (variation A); or execute a double threat
(variation B), which mates Black or wins his Rook. In (A), 1.
Qh8+ Kc7 2. **Qh2+** Kd8 allows 3. Qb8 mate, while 2. . . .Kc8 or
2. . . .Kc6 drops the Rook of 3. Qc2+.
   In (B), Black could try 1. . . .Rc1, but that ends in mate after 2.
Qb8+ Rc8 3. Qd6+ Ke8 4. Qe7. After 1. **Qb3 Re1+** 2. **Kd6**,
either he gets mated (2. . . .Ke8 and 2. . . .Rc1 are followed by
3. Qg8 mate) or drops the Rook (2. . . .Kc8 3. Qc3+).

	A	
1.	Qh8+	Kc7
2.	Qh2+	Kb7
3.	Qb2+	Ka7
4.	Qa3+	Kb7
5.	Qb3+	Kc6
6.	Qxd1	
	(1–0)	

	B	
1.	Qb3	Re1+
2.	Kd6	Ke8
3.	Qg8 mate	
	(1–0)	

ENDGAME 34

W: Ka1, Rf2 B: Kg6, Qb3
White moves and draws

Perpetual Attack 2

To have superior force is good. To exercise it wisely is better. Moving your Queen too close to the enemy King—squashing it—lays grounds for a stalemate. White draws by having his Rook perpetually attack the King along the 2nd rank. Starting with a Rook check on the f-file comes to an abrupt end: 1. Rf6+ Kg7 2. Rg6+ Kf7 3. Rg7+ Kf8 4. Rg8+ Qxg8, and the stalemate dissolves. If Black's King closes to attack the Rook, White checks anyway, for the Rook cannot be captured. And if Black's Queen takes the Rook after it moves to c2, that too is stalemate. Black cannot find safety along the sheltered b-file either, for White plays Rb2, pinning the Queen.

1. Rg2+ Kf5
2. Rf2+ Ke4
3. Re2+ Kd3
4. Rd2+ Kc4
5. Rc2+
   Draw

CHAPTER

4

Rooks and Minor Pieces

ENDGAME **35**

W: Kh1, Bh8 B: Kg3, Re7
White moves and draws

The Right-Corner Mate

Black threatens mate at e1 and a Bishop-King fork at h7—a double attack. If White had a light-square Bishop, his cause would be hopeless. But White has the dark-square Bishop, the right Bishop for the corner his King already occupies. To draw, the Bishop must move on squares of different color from the King's corner. Then it can block the Rook's check on a square contiguous to the King's. After 1. **Bd4 Re1+** 2. **Bg1**, Black has no way to progress, and carefully must keep White from a looming stalemate. In the final position, if everything were moved one square to the left, Black would force mate by making a tempo Rook move along the back rank. Such a move would force White's King to the corner and the Bishop (then at f1) would hang.

1. **Bd4   Re1+**
2. **Bg1   Rd1**
   Stalemate

ENDGAME 36

W: Kb6, Rb2 **B:** Kb8, Bf7
White moves and wins

Pin and Win

Black's Bishop controls the corner square closest to his King
(a8), therefore it's the wrong Bishop. To engineer a draw, the
Bishop must be able to occupy the square next to the corner
(here, b8). The actual corner square (a8) is reserved for Black's
King. If White's Rook attacks along the back row, Black's light-
square Bishop won't be a reliable shield for his King. The White
Rook conquers by starting with double attack, threatening the
Bishop and mate. After the x-ray assault 1. **Rf2**, White stam-
pedes the Bishop and the back-rank square immediately behind (f8). When the Rook reaches the last row, a delaying move
forces mate.

1.	Rf2	Be6
2.	Rf8 +	Bc8
3.	Rh8	Ka8
4.	Rxc8	mate

(1–0)

ENDGAME 37

W: Kg6, Rf7 B: Kg8, Bg1
White moves and wins

The Chase

Black's Bishop is free as a bird, but his King is confined to a dangerous corner. He could cope if trapped in light-square corners (a8 or h1) because his dark-square Bishop could shelter him from Rook-checks on an adjacent square. Should Black's King be driven to a dark-square corner (h8 or a1) however, the Bishop could not block checks if it were on the square next to the King. To set up a winning double attack, White must drive the free-as-a-bird Black Bishop into the open. The fireworks begin with 1. Rf1 Bh2 (curling up) 2. Rf2 Bg3 3. Rg2! This forces the Bishop into target range, since 3. . . . Bf4 and 3. . . . Bh4 both lose to discovered attack by White's King. After 3. . . . Bd6 (the best) White finishes by 4. Rd2 Be7 5. Rc2 Bd6 6. Rc8+ Bf8 7. Ra8+ (tempo) Kh8 8. Rxf8 mate.

1.	Rf1	Bh2	5. Rc2	Bd6
2.	Rf2	Bg3	6. Rc8+	Bf8
3.	Rg2	Bd6	7. Ra8+	Kh8
4.	Rd2	Be7	8. Rxf8	mate

(1–0)

ENDGAME **38**

W: Kd6, Rd7 B: Ke8, Bb6
White moves and wins

Corner Drive

Black's King has managed to avoid the noxious h8 corner, undoubtedly a plus. It's still on the edge of the board, however, and that spells trouble. After three forcing moves by White, suddenly Black's King is just where he doesn't want it to be: 1. **Ke6** (threatening 2. Rb7) **Kf8** (both 1. . . . Be3 2. Rd3, and 1. . . . Bf2 2. Rd2 let the Rook become menacing at the Bishop's expense) 2. **Rf7+ Kg8** (if 2. . . . Ke8, then 3. Rb7 is deadly) 3. **Kf6 Bd4+** 4. **Kg6 Bg1** 5. **Rf1 Bh2** 6. **Rf2 Bg3** 7. **Rg2** and wins. The Bishop has no refuge. Wherever it goes, a double attack follows.

1.	**Ke6**	**Kf8**
2.	**Rf7+**	**Kg8**
3.	**Kf6**	**Bd4+**
4.	**Kg6**	**Bg1**
5.	**Rf1**	**Bh2**
6,	**Rf2**	**Bg3**
7.	**Rg2**	

(1–0)

ENDGAME **39**

W: Kd1, Bg3 **B:** Ke3, Re2
White moves and draws

Positional Draw

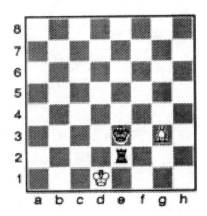

Consider the previous endgame with colors reversed and the defending side (White) to move. Facing the threatened 1. . . . Kd3, along with 2. . . . Rg2, White must choose to scurry his King, even though it's toward the dangerous sector: 1. **Kc1 Kd3** (Black pursues) 2. **Kb1**, and White's King still runs. If Black now could get his sire to c3 and Rook to c2, White would collapse. So Black continues 2. . . . **Kc3.** If instead he tries 2. . . . Rc2, then 3. Be5 shuts out Black's King. The Bishop then starts business on the a1-h8 diagonal, and Black no longer progresses. The star move is 3. **Kc1**! It seems a rare folly for White to move into vertical line with Black's King, but look sharp, for Black has *no way to take advantage. If he moves his Rook along the 2nd rank, White's Bishop can check from e5.* Meanwhile, after 3. . . . Re3, the Bishop temporizes to h4, retaining control of e1. Black is impassed and the result is a positional draw.

1. **Kc1   Kd3**
2. **Kb1   Kc3**
3. **Kc1**
Draw

ENDGAME **40**

W: Ke5, Rc6 **B:** Kb5, Ne8
White moves and wins

Separation

Generally, you err if you separate your Knight and King in such endings, for the horseman needs its majesty's aegis. The Rook does the restricting, confining, and driving. The King approaches or assumes a centralized post. The Rook moves in for the kill. The King, Rook, and Knight form a straight line in the final situation—a distinctive spike of pieces. Yes, a Knight on the rim is dim.

1. Rc8   Ng7
2. Rg8   Nh5
3. Rg5

(1–0)

ENDGAME 41

W: Kf8, Nh6 B: Ke6, Rh7
White moves and draws

Togetherness

Such a simple axiom: keep the Knight close to the King. Otherwise, the steed runs off the cliff. For example, if 1. Ng4, Black traps the Knight with 1 . . . . Rh3. The Knight is lost by a pin (2. Kg7 Rg3) or a fork (2. Nf2 Rf3 +), or White gets mated (2. Ke8 Rh8). But the retreat to g8 saves the day. The Knight is guarded, while Black's King is prevented from opposing White's at f6. No mate can be forced, the Knight can't be pinned or forked, and no real progress is possible. The best Black can do is 1. **Ng8 Rf7 +** 2. **Ke8 Ra7** 3. **Kf8 Rh7** 4. **Ke8 Rf7** (4 . . . . Rg7 5. Kf8 Rg6 6. Ne7) 5. **Nh6 Rf1,** giving White an opportunity to go wrong. If now 6. Kd8?, then . . . Rg1 7. Ke8 Rg6 8. Nf7 Rg8 is mate. But once again 6. **Ng8** puts White's house in order.

1.	Ng8	Rf7 +
2.	Ke8	Ra7
3.	Kf8	Rh7
4.	Ke8	Rf7
5.	Nh6	Rf1
6.	Ng8	
	Draw	

ENDGAME **42**

W: Kd6, Rf7, Bd5 B: Kc8, Re8
White moves and wins

Attacking the Weak Side

This is one of the positions originally analyzed by the studious Philidor, circa 1750. Sometimes situations of Rook and Bishop vs. Rook are a draw, others are a win for White. Unless Black's pieces are coordinated, he gets mated or loses his Rook. The secret is to play on Black's weak side, away from his strong side stalwart Rook! 1. **Ra7** (threatening mate) **Rd8+**   2. **Kc6 Kb8**   3. **Ra5 Rh8** (3 . . . Rd7   4. Kxc7? is a stalemate try, but it fails to 4. Rb5+ Kc8   5. Be6, pinning and winning the Rook)   4. **Kb6 Rh6+**   5. **Bc6 Rxc6+**   6. **Kxc6 Kc8**   7. **Ra8 mate.**

1.	Ra7	Rd8+
2.	Kc6	Kb8
3.	Ra5	Rh8
4.	Kb6	Rh6+
5.	Bc6	Rxc6+
6.	Kxc6	Kc8
7.	Ra8	mate

(1–0)

ENDGAME **43**

W: Kd6, Rf7, Bd5 B: Ke8, Re3
White moves and wins

Rook Lift 1

White strives to control the square e8. Check with the Bishop at c6 is in the air, but first White must find a haven for his Rook at f7. The key move is the Rook lift to the 4th rank, 1. **Rf4** (threatening 2. Bc6+ Kd8 3. Rf8+ Re8 4. Rxe8 mate). If Black pins the Bishop (1 . . . . Rd3), White plants his Rook on the g-file (2. Rg4) and Black cannot get back to block the upcoming back-rank check (f3 is held by the Bishop). Black must play 1. . . . **Kd8.** Now White reveals the secret of his first move, 2. **Be4!,** cutting off Black's Rook from the defense and threatening 3. Rf8 mate. Black has no choice; he must step onto the fatal square, 2. . . . **Ke8,** and White concludes 3. **Bc6+ Kd8 4. Rf8+ Re8 5. Rxe8 mate.**

1.	Rf4	Kd8
2.	Be4	Ke8
3.	Bc6+	Kd8
4.	Rf8+	Re8
5.	Rxe8	mate

(1–0)

ENDGAME 44

W: Kd6, Rf7, Bd5 B: Kd8, Re3
White moves and wins

Breaking Coordination

Black's forces are poised in delicate defensive balance, so White tips the scales with the disruptive 1. **Rd7+**. Black must commit to one side or the other. Queenside flight loses immediately (1. . . . Kc8 2. Ra7), thanks to the Bishop's watch over b3. Therefore 1. . . .**Ke8** 2. **Rb7** (a mate threat feint to further disturb Black's coordination) **Kf8** 3. **Rf7+ Ke8** (if 3. . . . Kg8, then 4. Rf3+ wins Black's Rook), and now the lift 4. **Rf4** decides as in the previous endgame.

1.	Rd7+	Ke8
2.	Rb7	Kf8
3.	Rf7+	Ke8
4.	Rf4	Kd8
5.	Be4	Ke8
6.	Bc6+	Kd8
7.	Rf8+	Re8
8.	Rxe8	mate

(1–0)

ENDGAME **45**

W: Kd6, Rf7, Bf3 B: Ke8, Re1
White moves and wins

Rook Lift 2

The Rook lift (1. **Rf4**) is mighty dangerous. It threatens a Bishop check at c6 and subsequent mate. Black's Rook is unable to counterattack White's King because the Bishop commands d1. It's the Bishop's day, first theatening mate by guarding e8, then commandeering the Queenside block-point c8. The overwrought Black pieces are done in.

1.	Rf4	Kd8
2.	Bh5	Kc8
3.	Rb4	Rc1
4.	Bg4 +	Kd8
5.	Rb8 +	Rc8
6.	Rxc8	mate

(1–0)

ENDGAME **46**

W: Kd6, Rg7, Bd5 **B**: Kd8, Re1
White moves and wins

Shifting Sides

With Black's Rook on e1, White wishes to get his Rook to f7 and his Bishop to f3. But it can't be done directly: (A) 1. Rf7 Re2 2. Bf3 Rd2 +, and the Bishop is obliged to return to d5 to block the check; (B) 1. Bf3 Ke8, and Black's King keeps the Rook out of f7. The day is saved by shifting White's Rook from Kingside to Queenside and back again, starting with 1. **Ra7**, threatening mate. Black must hie his own Rook to the Queenside to shield against mate, 1. . . . **Rc1**, but that lets White's Rook reach the desired square with tempo, 2. **Rf7**, because it now menaces mate at f8. So Black's Rook comes back to the Kingside, 2. . . . **Re1** (the alternative, 2. . . . Ke8, loses after 3. Rf4 Rd1 4. Rb4 Kf8 5. Rg4, and mate at g8 follows). White's Bishop now reaches its goal too, 3. **Bf3**, and Black's Rook cannot attack from d1. If 3. . . . Ke8, then 4. Rf4 transforms into an earlier endgame; and if instead, 3 . . . Re8, then Black buckles, 4. Ra7. Relatively best is 3. . . . **Re3**, but after 4. **Bc6 Rd3 +** 5. **Bd5**, Black again founders for a move. If he tries 5 . . . . Ke8, he is totally uncoordinated after 6. Rg7; and if 5. . . . Re3, then 6. **Rd7 +** leads into an earlier losing endgame in this series.

1. **Ra7**	**Rc1**		4. **Bc6**	**Rd3 +**
2. **Rf7**	**Re1**		5. **Bd5**	**Re3**
3. **Bf3**	**Re3**		6. **Rd7 +**	

(1–0)

ENDGAME 47

W: Kd6, Rf1, Bd5 B: Kd8, Re7
White moves and wins

Philidor's Position

In this famous position, Black threatens to Rook-check White's King from d7. White dare not oppose this by 1. Bc6 (or 1. Be6), for 1. . . . Rd7+ 2. Bxd7 is stalemate. White instead checks on the last row to force Black's Rook off the 7th rank, 1. **Rf8+ Re8.** Now with 2. **Rf7,** White takes control of the 7th rank for himself. Black's best try is 2. . . . **Re2,** setting up a possible check from behind at d2 on a square that cannot be guarded by White's Bishop. However, after the tempo move, 3. **Rg7,** Black's Rook must commit to e1 or e3, where the checks from the rear (at d1 or d3) can be controlled by the Bishop. Victory then follows, as in the preceding endgames.

1.	Rf8+	Re8	9.	Rd7+	Ke8
2.	Rf7	Re2	10.	Rb7	Kf8
3.	Rg7	Re1	11.	Rf7+	Ke8
4.	Ra7	Rc1	12.	Rf4	Kd8
5.	Rf7	Re1	13.	Be4	Ke8
6.	Bf3	Re3	14.	Bc6+	Kd8
7.	Bc6	Rd3+	15.	Rf8+	Re8
8.	Bd5	Re3	16.	Rxe8	mate

(1–0)

PART
TWO

The Pawns in Action

This section belongs to the one and only pawn. The ability of the unflappable foot soldier to be promoted to a position of power upon reaching the 8th rank gives it sufficient force to mate. And this mere varlet, as a passed pawn with no hostile neighbors in its path to the Queening square, is truly a foe to be reckoned with. All stops must be pulled out to prevent the dangerous passed pawn from reaching Queensland.

The rule of the square, the cornerstone of all King-and-pawn endgame theory, determines the outcome when the passed pawn alone grapples with the enemy King. The picture becomes more complex when both Kings enter the fray. Here very precise terminology is necessary to fully and accurately describe the full range of movement employed in the duel of the two Kings vying with each other over the chessboard. Terms such as *opposition, triangulation, squeeze,* and so on embody fundamental concepts characterizing various aspects of the exclusive, nuanced realm of monarchical combat.

Theoreticians have tried to subsume the whole range of larger aspects of the endgame struggle into a single theoretical superstructure. The theory of corresponding squares, the most recent attempt, is too new and untried. Many of its details still remain to be worked out. More practical and successful is the German *zugzwang* (meaning "movebound"), which distills to one word the vast strategic network of endgame positions. In *zugzwang* situations, the obligation to make a move, normally an advantage, becomes a crushing burden. The side whose turn it is must yield ground to the adversary, often with fatal consequences.

Part Two presents all the basic concepts common to King-and-pawn endings, explained in words and illustrated by examples. Each concept is given initially in its simplest, most un-diluted form, and then later integrated with other themes. This directory of ideal leads in turn to an appreciation of the richly intricate patterns emerging on a chessboard so empty of other chessmen.

5

King and Pawn vs. King

ENDGAME **48**

W: Kh1, Pa2 B: Kg8
White moves and wins

Square of the Pawn

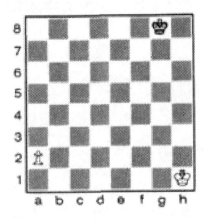

A King can overtake a speeding passed pawn two ways. One method is to compare the number of moves it takes for the pawn and King to reach the Queening square. If it's the same, the pawn is caught; if the pawn needs less, it Queens. Another method is to visualize the "square of the pawn." After the pawn moves to a4, imagine a box of twenty squares, from a4 to a8 to e8 to e4. Black's King must be able to enter that box on the move to catch the pawn on a diagonal in to the back rank. In the diagram, the pawn starts on the 2nd rank, and the box apparently runs from a2 to a8 to g8 to g2, with Black's King already in the box. But remember, a pawn may advance two squares on its first move. To compensate, the box must be drawn as though the a-pawn were starting on a3. In this case, Black's King languishes in the outlands.

1. a4   Kf7
2. a5   Ke6
3. a6   Kd6
4. a7   Kc7
5. a8/Q
   (1–0)

ENDGAME **49**

W: Kc6 B: Ka8, Ph5
White moves and draws

Stepping into the Square

In this setup, the square extends from h5 to d1 to d5. White enters it at d5 immediately. A visual shortcut is to draw an imaginary diagonal line from the pawn to the back rank— here, h5 to d1. The d-file then becomes the line White's King must cross. It does so on the move. The diagonal containing White's King and the h1 promotion square is the "critical diagonal." In the diagram it is d5-e4-f3-g2-h1. Retreating the King along a critical diagonal can be cardinal to an endgame's solution. The defender uses the path to get back quickly, and the attacker tries to obstruct it.

1.	Kd5	h4
2.	Ke4	h3
3.	Kf3	h2
4.	Kg2	h1/Q+
5.	K×h1	
	Draw	

ENDGAME **50**

W: Kb6, Pa2 **B:** Kd7
White moves and wins

Clearing the Path

Black's King could hunker on c8, obtaining a draw. White has enough material to win (the pawn could become a new Queen), yet he cannot force promotion once Black's King is on c8. Even if White's King moved to a7, thwarting Black's King from reaching the corner, he would block the advance of his own pawn, while Black's King from c8 or c7 denies him egress. Now the "critical square" b7 becomes important. If it is occupied by White's King, White wins, for the pawn proceeds forward unchallenged. If Black's King reaches c8, however, White's King cannot occupy b7, the a-pawn's critical square. In King and pawn versus King endings, a square is critical if, by occupying it, the superior side's King could ensure the promotion of the passed pawn. A pawn is "passed" when no enemy pawn obstructs its path to the promotion square or guards a square it must pass over. Loosely, a passed pawn has "passed" all opposing pawns.

1.	Kb7	Kd6	3.	a5	Kb5
2.	a4	Kc5	4.	a6	

(1–0)

ENDGAME **51**

W: Kg5, Pa2 B: Kf3
White moves and wins

Shielding Off

Black to play can draw with a Kingly move to e4 or e3, getting within the "square of White's advancing a-pawn," which extends from a3 to a8 to f8 to f3. This prevents White from winning by a straight pawn march. After 1. a4 Ke4, Black is in the "square of the pawn" (now imagined from a4 to a8 to e8 to e4) and on the critical retreating diagonal (e4-d5-c6-b7-a8), enabling Black's King to get back in time. If White goes first, the win is achieved by White's King opposing Black's, row by row, across the board to the Queenside, shielding off Black's King from entering the "square of the pawn." The turning point comes when White's King is on c5 and Black's on c3. Unable to move to b3 because White's pawn guards that square, Black gives way to b2. White's pawn then utilizes its two-square option to get beyond Black's grasp.

1. Kf5   Ke3
2. Ke5   Kd3
3. Kd5   Kc3
4. Kc5   Kb2
5. a4

(1–0)

ENDGAME **52**

W: Kg6, Pf6 B: Kf8
White moves and wins

The Squeeze

Black has his King on the Queening square, but the simple advance 1. f7 squeezes him out. Black's King must exit to the left, 1. . . . Ke7, allowing White's King to enter on the right. The move 2. Kg7 takes control of the Queening square, and after 3. e8/Q, White mates within ten moves. The key to this ending is timing the advance of the pawn to the 7th rank without check. You "squeeze" your opponent's King when you force it off the back row by pushing your pawn to the 7th rank without giving check. Generally, if you are being "squeezed," you must make a move that worsens your position.

1.	f7	Ke7	6.	Kf5	Kc6
2.	Kg7	Kd6	7.	Ke6	Kc7
3.	f8/Q +	Kd5	8.	Qb5	Kc8
4.	Qb4	Kc6	9.	Kd6	Kd8
5.	Kf6	Kd5	10.	Qd7	mate

(1–0)

ENDGAME **53**

W: Kf1 **B:** Kg3, Pf3
White moves and draws

Opposing

The other side of the coin. If Black's pawn advances to the 7th rank with check, the defense holds. White, on move, mus⁺ decide whether to put his King on e1 or g1. It works out nicely after 1. Ke1 if Black cooperates and pushes his pawn with check: 1. . . . f2+ 2. Kf1 Kf3. But after the correct response, 1. . . . Kg2, the pawn owns a safe conduct to the Queening square. White, therefore, must play 1. **Kg1**, opposing Black's intentions. Now when the pawn steps forward, 1. . . . **f2+**, it is with check and stalemate results from 2. **Kf1 Kf3**. By opposing Black's King, White's King cannot be squeezed.

1. **Kg1** f2+
2. **Kf1** Kf3
Stalemate

ENDGAME 54

W: Kd5, Pe6 B: Kd8
White moves and wins

Oppositional Squeeze

When Kings are on the same row with one square between them, occupying squares of the same color, they are "in opposition." The side *not* on the move has the advantage, and is said to "have the opposition." If White's King has the opposition, he controls the situation and can force his pawn ahead successfully. If Black's King has the opposition, he can stop White on the spot and draw. When the Kings stand in opposition, neither player desires to move, for that would give ground to his opponent. Therefore, the only sure way White can lay down a winning squeeze is to take the opposition on the d-file, 1. Kd6. The rules compel Black to move, and his King must give way. The side step 1. . . . Ke8, permits the unimpeded advance with advance 2. e7 and 3. e8/Q. And after 1. . . . Ke8, White squeezes with 2. e7 (no check), when Black is obliged to open the door to White's king: 2. . . . Kf7 3. Kc7 and 4. e8/Q.

1. Kd6	Ke8	6. Qe4	Kg5
2. e7	Kf7	7. Ke6	Kh6
3. Kd7	Kf6	8. Kf6	Kh5
4. e8/Q	Kf5	9. Qd4	Kh6
5. Qe3	Kf6	10. Qh4	mate

(1–0)

ENDGAME **55**

Diagonal Squeeze

The Kings "stand in opposition" when they sit on same color squares and are separated by an odd number of squares (1, 3, or 5) along the same straight row (a rank, file, or diagonal). When Kings in opposition occupy the same file, the Kings are in "vertical opposition." If they occupy the same rank, they are in "horizontal opposition." And if lined up on the same diagonal, they are in "diagonal opposition." If they are separated by one square, the opposition is called "direct." If there are three squares between the two Kings, the opposition is "distant." If the separation is five squares, the opposition is "long distant." With the upward 1. **Kb6**, White takes the direct diagonal opposition, and after 1. . . . **Kc8**, edges by 2. **c7 Kd7** 3. **Kb7 Kd6** 4. **c8/Q**. Mate soon follows.

1.	Kb6	Kc8	6.	Kc6	Kf6
2.	c7	Kd7	7.	Kd6	Kf7
3.	Kb7	Kd6	8.	Qg5	Kf8
4.	c8/Q	Kd5	9.	Ke6	Ke8
5.	Qg4	Ke5	10.	Qe7	mate

(1–0)

ENDGAME 56

W: Ka5, Pc6 B: Ka8
White moves and wins

Vertical Squeeze

Black's King is not on the Queening square, but it is within the "square of the pawn," (c6 to c8 to a8 to a6) so the hasty thrust 1. c7? ends in capture after 1. . . . Kb7. The pawn's forward motion requires royal support. Only choice of the right squares for advancement, and precise timing will secure White's eventual victory. For example, 1. Kb6? is a mistake. After 1. . . . Kb8, the pawn can reach the 7th rank only with check, and Black draws by 2. c7+ Kc8 3. Kc6 stalemate. The only correct step for White is to move his King in line with Black's, one square separating the two monarchs, so they stand in direct vertical opposition. With 1. Ka6, White seizes the direct vertical opposition on the a-file. After 1. . . . Kb8 2. Kb6 Kc8 the squeeze is on: 3. c7 Kd7 4. Kb7 and Queens on the next move. If instead of 2. . . . Kc8, Black plays 2. . . . Ka8, White must avoid the trap 3. c7 stalemate, opting for 3. Kc7 Ka7 4. Kd7, and the pawn is convoyed to the Queening square.

1. Ka6	Kb8	5. c8/Q	Ke5	9. Kb6	Kd7
2. Kb6	Kc8	6. Qg4	Kd5	10. Qe5	Kd8
3. c7	Kd7	7. Qf4	Kc5	11. Kc6	Kc8
4. Kb7	Kd6	8. Qe4	Kd6	12. Qc7	mate

(1–0)

ENDGAME **57**

W: Ke2 B: Ke4, Pe3
White moves and draws

Frontal Defense

Black's pawn dwells on its 6th rank and his King lurks behind on its 5th. A bad sign. White's King is poised perfectly for defense: on the blockade square e2, immediately in front of the pawn. That's a clear draw. White simply shifts between e2 and e1. If Black's King moves up a rank, White's King directly opposes him (1. . . .Kd3 2. Kd1, or 1. . . .Kf3 2. Kf1), taking the direct vertical opposition. No progress is possible. In such cases, moving the pawn to its 7th rank with check only draws, for it no longer is possible to squeeze White's King out. Stalemate ensues.

1. **Ke1** Kd3
2. **Kd1** d2 +
3. **Ke1** Ke3
   Stalemate

ENDGAME **58**

W: Kg5, Pe6 B: Kg7
White moves and wins

Transition to a Squeeze

Black has the direct vertical opposition, but he can't maintain it. The move 1. **Kf5** is forced (for anything else loses the e-pawn). Relatively best is 1. . . .**Kg8**, giving White a chance to go wrong. White continues 2. **Kg6!**. But not 2. Kf6?, for 2. . . .Kf8, regaining the opposition, draws. So 2. . . .**Kf8** 3. **Kf6 Ke8** leads to the pawn squeeze 4. **e7**, which drives Black's King from the Queening square: 4. . . .**Kd7** 5. **Kf7**.

1. Kf5	Kg8	7. Qa4	Kc5
2. Kg6	Kf8	8. Ke6	Kb6
3. Kf6	Ke8	9. Kd6	Kb7
4. e7	Kd7	10. Qa5	Kb8
5. Kf7	Kd6	11. Kc6	Kc8
6. e8/Q	Kd5	12. Qc7 mate	

(1–0)

ENDGAME **59**

W: Kh2 **B:** Kf3, Pg3
White moves and draws

Stalemate

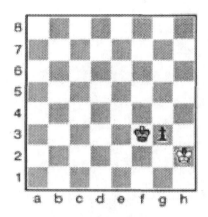

Let's say you have an extra Knight-pawn, your King is sitting on the 6th or 7th rank ahead of the pawn, and it's your move. Be cautious about pushing your pawn. It may be better to waste time and reposition your King to a more recognizable situation, even transferring it to the Rook-file in some cases, to avoid helping your opponent to set pawn-baited stalemate traps. You cannot afford to be imprecise with a pawn. Sometimes, after a bad piece move, you can return to where you started. But pawns can't move backward. Black has erroneously pushed his pawn to the 6th, allowing White to draw with a frontal defense variation (see Endgame 57). After 1. **Kh1**, 1. . . .Kf2 stalemates. Black should have continued his pawn on to g4 and played his King to f2 instead, then to g3 followed by h3. That combination would have sprung any stalemate snares.

1. **Kh1** **g2 +**
2. **Kg1** **Kg3**
Stalemate

ENDGAME **60**

W: Ke6, Pf5 B: Kf8
White moves and wins

Direct Opposition

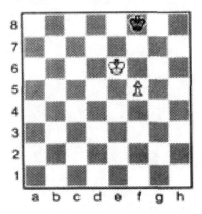

White would err if he pushed his pawn, for Black's King would then oppose White's, taking the direct vertical opposition, ending in a draw. White instead should seize the opposition, 1. **Kf6.** Then Black's King must accede, allowing White's King a turning maneuver to the 7th rank to guard the squares in the pawn's path. This kind of transitional opposition, firmly clearing the way for follow-up turning maneuvers that assure a win, is the most powerful there is. These stratagems permit White's King to occupy the pawn's critical squares, which are two ranks ahead of pawns on the 2nd, 3rd, or 4th ranks, but only one rank in front of a pawn on the 5th rank. Thus, if his pawn is on the 3rd rank, White's King must be able to occupy one of three critical squares on the 5th rank. These three squares are found on three adjoining files: the file with the pawn and the two adjacent files. Together these three files constitute the pawn's "universe." Generally, it is to neither King's advantage to move outside the universe. If White gets the opposition within the universe he can apply a turning maneuver to occupy a critical square to squeeze out his opponent's King.

1.	Kf6	Ke8
2.	Kg7	Ke7
3.	f6+	Ke6
4.	f7	Kd5
5.	f8/Q	Kc4
6.	Qa3	Kd4
7.	Kf6	Ke4
8.	Qc3	Kd5
9.	Kf5	Kd6
10.	Qc4	Kd7
11.	Qc5	Ke8
12.	Ke6	Kd8
13.	Qc3	Ke8
14.	Qh8 mate	

(1–0)

ENDGAME **61**

W: Kd5, Pc5 B: Kb7
White moves and wins

Critical Squares

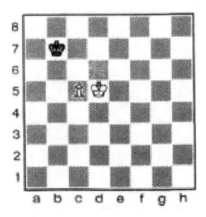

Critical squares for pawns on the 5th rank are one row ahead of the pawn—not two, as seen with pawns on the 2nd, 3rd, and 4th ranks. That's because as White's pawn and King advance to the higher ranks, Black's King is forced to the back row, where it runs out of maneuvering room. White's critical squares here are d6, c6, and b6. If White's King can occupy any of these three squares, he can force a win, whatever Black does. If Black can prevent White's King from getting to these squares while White's pawn is still on the 5th rank, Black draws. Thus, if Black goes first, he draws by 1. . . .Kc7. But if White moves first, he can precede his pawn to the 6th and occupy the critical square, d6. This is what most King-and-pawn vs. King battles are about: getting the stronger side's King to the 6th rank in front of the pawn. Once you accomplish that, you win whether the pawn (if not a Rook-pawn) occupies the 2nd, 3rd, 4th, or 5th ranks. You should not move your pawn to the 6th rank unless your King is already on the 6th rank and the advance takes the opposition, allowing Black's King to be squeezed.

1.	Kd6	Kc8
2.	Kc6	Kb8
3.	Kd7	Kb7
4.	c6+	Kb6
5.	c7	Kc5
6.	c8/Q+	Kd4
7.	Ke6	Ke4
8.	Qc3	Kf4
9.	Qd3	Kg4
10.	Qe3	Kh5
11.	Kf5	Kh4
12.	Qc3	Kh5
13.	Qh8 mate	

(1–0)

ENDGAME 62

W: Kf7, Pg5 B: Kh8
White moves and wins

Knight-Pawn Trap

White's King has reached a critical square and beyond, for it is sufficient for White's King to occupy the 6th rank to win. It appears that the g-pawn has all the makings of a new Queen. Yet, the Black King's proximity to the board's edge sets a nasty trap, 1. g6 stalemate. The winning idea is for White to retrace his steps, stationing his own king on h6, preventing Black's King from using the h-file to set up a stalemate trick and forcing it out of the corner.

1. Kg6	Kg8	8. Kg6	Ke5
2. Kh6	Kh8	9. Kg5	Kd6
3. g6	Kg8	10. Kf6	Kd7
4. g7	Kf7	11. Qc5	Kd8
5. Kh7	Kf6	12. Qa7	Kc8
6. g8/Q	Ke5	13. Ke6	Kd8
7. Qc4	Kd6	14. Qb8 mate	

(1–0)

ENDGAME 63

W: Ka1 B: Kb5, Pc5
White moves and wins

Distant Opposition

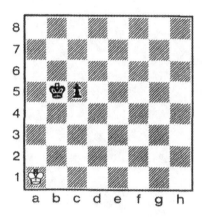

Black's King clearly can take a position in front of his pawn, a pluperfect plus. But with his pawn on its 4th rank Black's King must be able to occupy the critical squares on its 6th rank. Surely, if White is impetuous, Black succeeds: 1. Kb2? Kb4 (taking the direct opposition) 2. Kc2 Kc4 3. Kd2 Kb3(the turning maneuver) 4. Kc1 Kc3 5. Kd1 Kb2 6. Kd2 c4, and the pawn is handed through. With precision play, however, White on the move seizes the distant vertical opposition, 1. Kb1, positioning his King an odd number of squares away from Black's King—three—on the same file, keeping it at bay. By maintaining, from move to move, some form of opposition (either distant vertical or direct vertical), White can prevent Black's King from reaching a critical square.

1.	Kb1	Kb4	5.	Kc2	c3
2.	Kb2	Kc4	6.	Kc1	Kd3
3.	Kc2	Kd4	7.	Kd1	c2 +
4.	Kd2	c4	8.	Kc1	Kc3
				Stalemate	

ENDGAME 64

W: Ke4, Pd4 **B:** Kf8
White moves and wins

Outside Critical Square

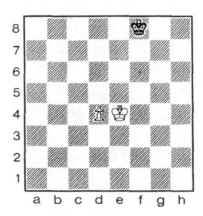

The three critical squares in front of White's 4th-rank pawn are
e6, d6, and c6. White can seize only one of them: c6, the
outside critical square. The "outside critical square" is the one
farthest from the enemy King. Whenever the attacking King has
an option, it is better to head for the outside critical square,
which tends to be harder for Black's King to reach. Here,
White's King diagonally beelines (e4-d5-c6) for the outside critical square, crossing over in front of his pawn, a maneuver
known as "the overpass."

1.	Kd5	Ke7
2.	Kc6	Kd8
3.	Kd6	Kc8
4.	Ke7	Kc7
5.	d5	Kc8
6.	d6	Kb7
7.	d7	Kc6
8.	d8/Q	

(1–0)

ENDGAME 65

W: Kb2, Pe4 B: Ka8
White moves and wins

Extended Overpass

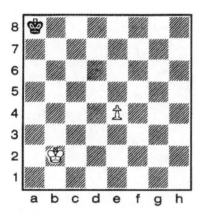

An inadequate winning try is 1. Kb3?, which is answered by either 1. ... Kb7 (or even 1. ... Kb8). Both moves obstruct White's King from reaching its critical squares on the 6th rank (d6, e6, or f6). But White can force destiny's hand with a long overpass to f6, the outside critical square. Then the pawn is convoyed home.

1.	Kc3	Kb7
2.	Kd4	Kc6
3.	Ke5	Kd7
4.	Kf6	Ke8
5.	Ke6	Kf8
6.	Kd7	Kf7
7.	e5	Kf8
8.	e6	Kg7
9.	e7	Kf6
10.	e8/Q	

(1–0)

ENDGAME **66**

W: Ke1, Pg4 **B**: Kc8
White moves and wins

The Underpass 1

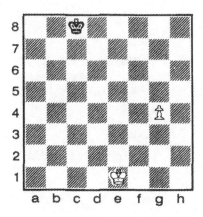

In this example, a pawn push draws, for Black's King gets to the crucial area before White's. A direct advance by White's King 1. Ke2 is stymied by 1. . . . Kd7 2. Ke3 Ke7! (distant vertical opposition) 3. Kf4 Kf6. Once again, the riddle is solved by heading for the outside critical square (here, h6). To get there, White's King executes the underpass, sliding behind his pawn: e1-f2-g3-h4.

1.	Kf2	Kd7		
2.	Kg3	Ke6		
3.	Kh4	Kf6		
4.	Kh5	Kg7		
5.	Kg5	Kh7		
6.	Kf6	Kh8		

7.	Kg6	Kg8	
8.	g5	Kh8	
9.	Kf7	Kh7	
10.	g6 +	Kh6	
11.	g7	Kg5	
12.	g8/Q		

(1–0)

ENDGAME **67**

W: Kd3 **B:** Kc5, Pc6
White moves and draws

Opposition

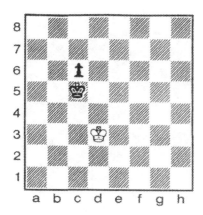

White marks time, frustrating the hostile intentions of Black's King by 1. **Kc3** taking direct opposition. After 1. . . . **Kd5** 2. **Kd3,** Black proceeds solely by advancing his pawn: 2. . . . **c5** 3. **Kc3 c4.** White now must surrender the blockading square c3. In principle, he ought to withdraw to the reserve blockading square c2, immediately behind the blockading square c3. By 4. **Kc2 Kd4** 5. **Kd2,** White shuts Black's King out of his critical 6th-rank squares.

1.	Kc3	Kd5
2.	Kd3	c5
3.	Kc3	c4
4.	Kc2	Kd4
5.	Kd2	c3 +
6.	Kc2	Kc4
7.	Kc1	Kb3
8.	Kb1	c2 +
9.	Kc1	Kc3
	Stalemate	

ENDGAME 68

W: Kg5, Pg3 B: Kg7
White moves and wins

Reserve Tempo

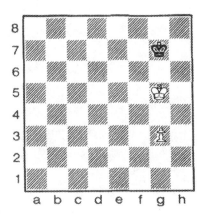

White's King grips a critical square (g5), so he must have a winning game. Black has the direct vertical opposition, but only temporarily. Utilizing his reserve tempo, White advances his pawn, transferring the move to Black and gaining the opposition for himself. After 1. **g4**, Black gives ground, 1. . . . **Kh7**, and White's King ascends the board with a turning maneuver, 2. **Kf6**, occupying a critical square in the process. The ending echoes several we've already seen.

1.	g4	Kh7
2.	Kf6	Kh8
3.	Kg6	Kg8
4.	g5	Kh8
5.	Kf7	Kh7
6.	g6+	Kh6
7.	g7	Kg5
8.	g8/Q+	
	(1–0)	

ENDGAME **69**

W: Kc1, Pb3 B: Ke8
White moves and wins

The Underpass 2

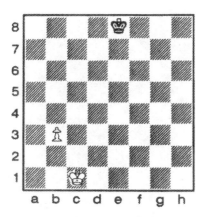

Another underpass. White's King gets to a3 as quickly as he does to c3, and by a diagonal march to a3, he gains ground on Black's King. Black stops the White King's dash for the outside critical square (a5) by lunging to b6, but with Kb4, White grasps hold of the direct vertical opposition, reaching a critical square on the next move.

1. Kb2	Kd7	9. b5	Kb8
2. Ka3	Kc6	10. Kb6	Ka8
3. Ka4	Kb6	11. Kc7	Ka7
4. Kb4	Ka6	12. b6+	Ka8
5. Kc5	Kb7	13. b7+	Ka7
6. Kb5	Kc7	14. b8/Q+	Ka6
7. Ka6	Kc6	15. Qb6	mate
8. b4	Kc7	(1–0)	

ENDGAME **70**

W: Ka3, Pg2 B: Kb5
White moves and wins

Maintaining the Opposition

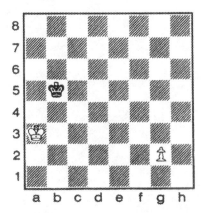

The pawn can't do for itself: 1. g4 Kc5 (stepping into the "square of the pawn") 2. g5 Kd5 3. g6 Ke6 4. g7 Kf7 catches the pawn. White's King must seize the direct vertical opposition and maintain it, line by line across the board to the g-file. At that point, Black must give way, left or right, allowing White's King a turning maneuver to occupy a 4th-rank critical square (f4 or h4). Critical-square sets are two ranks ahead of their pawns on the 2nd, 3rd, or 4th ranks. This means the critical squares for a White pawn on g2 are f4, g4, and h4. By occupying any of these three squares, White's King will be able to promote his passed pawn by force.

1. Kb3	Kc5	8. Kg4	Kf6	15. Kf7	Kh7
2. Kc3	Kd5	9. Kh5	Kg7	16. g6+	Kh8
3. Kd3	Ke5	10. Kg5	Kf7	17. g7+	Kh7
4. Ke3	Kf5	11. Kh6	Kg8	18. g8/Q+	Kh6
5. Kf3	Kg5	12. Kg6	Kh8	19. Qg6	mate
6. Kg3	Kf5	13. g4	Kg8	(1–0)	
7. Kh4	Kg6	14. g5	Kh8		

W: Ke1, Pe2 B: Ke8
White moves and wins

Critical Squares #2

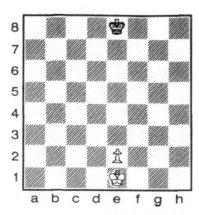

Everything depends on who moves. If Black goes first, his King can stop White's from occupying a 4th-rank critical square, two rows in front of the e-pawn (d4, e4, or f4). For example, 1. ...Ke7 (long-distant vertical opposition) 2. Kd2 Kd6 (distant vertical opposition) 3. Ke3 Ke5 (direct opposition), and Black draws. But if White goes first, he wins because he always gets to a 4th-rank critical square: Kd2-e3-e4 (or to d4 or f4).

1. Kd2	Kd8	8. e5	Ke8
2. Ke3	Ke7	9. Ke6	Kf8
3. Ke4	Ke6	10. Kd7	Kf7
4. e3	Kd6	11. e6+	Kf8
5. Kf5	Kd5	12. e7+	Kf7
6. e4+	Kd6	13. e8/Q+	
7. Kf6	Kd7	(1–0)	

ENDGAME **72**

W: Kc1 B: Kc8, Pc7
White plays and draws

Long-Distant Opposition

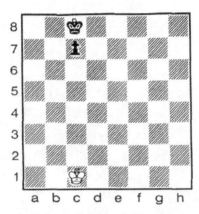

Black moves and wins as White did in the previous endgame. But White, with the move, draws by blocking Black from reaching his pawn's critical squares. To win with the pawn at c7, Black's King must be set to occupy either b5, c5, or d5. White starts by taking the long-distant vertical opposition, 1. **Kc2**. Both Kings now stand on the same color squares (light), separated by an odd number of squares (five) along the row they are on (the c-file). After 1. . . .Kb7 2. **Kb3**, the Kings stand in distant vertical opposition, and White's has the advantage because he moves second. Finally, with 2. . . .Kc6 3. **Kc4**, White holds the direct opposition, and Black can't attain any of his critical squares. Black's King can move up later, but only after moving his pawn, which changes the critical squares, pushing them even further beyond Black's King.

1.	Kc2	Kb7	7.	Kd3	c4+	13. Kd1	c2+
2.	Kb3	Kc6	8.	Kc3	Kc5	14. Kc1	Kc3
3.	Kc4	Kd6	9.	Kc2	Kb4		Stalemate
4.	Kd4	c6	10.	Kb2	c3+		
5.	Kc4	c5	11.	Kc2	Kc4		
6.	Kc3	Kd5	12.	Kc1	Kd3		

ENDGAME 73

W: Kf1 **B:** Kg3, Ph3
White moves and draws

Rook-Pawn Draws

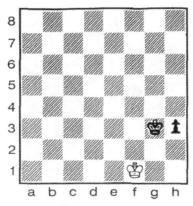

White draws in the simplest manner: he installs his King on the Queening square and shuttles back and forth between h1 and g1. Any attempt to eject him produces stalemate. If Black moves first, he wins by pushing his h-pawn. In most cases, however, Black's King has to occupy g2, his h-pawn's critical square, in order to win. That prevents White's King from getting to the corner, or even the square f1. A different critical square formula exists for Rook-pawns. The critical square for any Rook-pawn is found in the 7th rank of the adjacent Knight-file. Thus, for a White pawn on a2, a3, a4, or a5, for example, the critical square is b7. Only by occupying that square can White's King guarantee the unblemished march of his a-pawn.

1. **Kg1** h2 +
2. **Kh1** Kh3
   Stalemate

ENDGAME **74**

W: Kd2 **B:** Kb3, Pa5
White moves and draws

Controlling the Critical Square

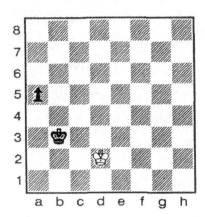

Black to play wins by moving his King to his a-pawn's critical square, 1. . . .Kb2. It's critical because, if Black's King can occupy it, White's King cannot achieve the corner or impede the a-pawn's advance. Occupation of a critical square means that the pawn can be promoted by force, even against the best defense. But if White plays first, he gets his King to c1. Black's King never gains his critical square and the pawn is thwarted.

A	
1. **Kc1**	a4
2. **Kb1**	a3
3. **Ka1**	a2
Stalemate	

B	
1. **Kc1**	Ka2
2. **Kc2**	a4
3. **Kc1**	a3
4. **Kc2**	Ka1
5. **Kc1**	a2
6. **Kc2**	
Stalemate	

ENDGAME **75**

W: Kf4 B: Kh1, Ph3
White moves and draws

Rear Defense

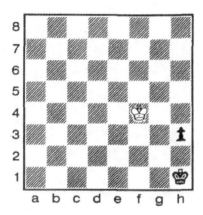

White bounds back just in time to stalemate Black. After 1. **Kg3**, Black has no way to keep his pawn except to push it to h2. But then White retreats his King farther to f2, and Black, the superior side, is stalemated.

1. **Kg3**   **h2**
2. **Kf2**
   Stalemate

CHAPTER

6

King and Two Pawns vs. King

ENDGAME 76

W: Kc6, Pb6, Pb5 B: Kb8
White moves and wins

Pawn Pitch 1

You have "doubled pawns" if two of your pawns occupy the same file because of a capture. Doubled pawns tend to be weak, since they can't protect each other as can "connected pawns" on adjacent files. But when you have doubled pawns and your opponent has nothing, generally you win. Whenever you need to tempo, the rear doubled pawn could be pushed one square (if there is a space between), making it your opponent's turn. An exception is doubled pawns on the Rook-file. Regardless of who gets the opposition in that case, Black still draws if his King blockades the Rook-pawns on the corner square. Here, the only possible lurking snafu is stalemate, which occurs after 1. **b7 Ka7** 2. Kc7?. But by "pitching," or sacrificing, his pawn instead, 2. **b8/Q+**, White avoids the draw and wins, for his King already sits on a critical square (c6) after the pawn is sacrificed.

1.	b7	Ka7	5. b6+	Ka8
2.	b8/Q+	Kxb8	6. b7+	Ka7
3.	Kb6	Ka8	7. b8/Q+	Ka6
4.	Kc7	Ka7	8. Qb6	mate

(1–0)

ENDGAME **77**

W: Kb3, Pb5, Pb4 **B:** Kb7
White moves and wins

King Dance

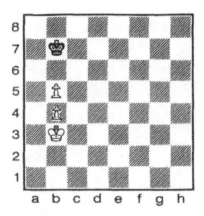

White's King is heading for c5. But he must avoid moving it to c4 before Black plays his King to b6, for that will lose the front pawn. White's King thereupon snakes around c4 (going from b3 to c3 to d4 to c5), retaining the possibility of defending his front pawn from c4 if Black attacks it: 1. **Kc3 Kc7** 2. **Kd4 Kb6.** Now 3. **Kc4** is in order, as Black has played his King to b6, threatening to capture the front pawn. After the moves 3. . . . **Kc7** 4. **Kc5 Kb7** 5. **b6**, Black sets a trap with 5. . . . **Ka6**, hoping for 6. Kc6 stalemate. But by ditching his lead pawn, 6. **b7**, White averts stalemate, takes the opposition after the b-pawn's capture, and reaches the critical squares on the 6th rank. He could afford to sacrifice the lead pawn because he still has one left.

1.	Kc3	Kc7	7.	Kb5	Ka7	13.	b7	Kc7
2.	Kd4	Kb6	8.	Kc6	Kb8	14.	Ka7	Kc6
3.	Kc4	Kc7	9.	Kb6	Ka8	15.	b8/Q	
4.	Kc5	Kb7	10.	b5	Kb8		(1–0)	
5.	b6	Ka6	11.	Ka6	Ka8			
6.	b7	Kxb7	12.	b6	Kb8			

ENDGAME **78**

W: Kg6, Pg7, Ph6 **B:** Kg8
White mates in one move

Pawn Mate

A basic position. White's King and connected pawns form a cohesive mating block. Sometimes the final position evolves from a pawn race, in which Black Queens a pawn before White but gets mated afterwards. The diagram could also result after a White capture on g7, when a white pawn on f6 captures on g7, checking Black's King on h8 and forcing it to g8.

1. **h7 mate**
(1–0)

ENDGAME 79

W: Kd5, Pb6, Pa7 B: Kb7
White moves and wins

Pawn Pitch 2

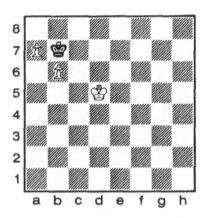

White has to ditch a pawn, else he could walk into stalemate; for example, 1. Kd6 Ka8 2. Kc7. The culprit is White's a-pawn, which is really superfluous. By sacrificing it, 1. a8/Q+ Kxa8, White's King can enter the fray safely with 2. Kc6, taking the direct diagonal opposition as his King lands on the 6th rank. With stalemate no longer a question, White wins through the usual escorting method.

1. a8/Q+	Kxa8
2. Kc6	Kb8
3. b7	Ka7
4. Kc7	Ka6
5. b8/Q	Ka5
7. Qb3	Ka6
8. Qb6	mate

(1–0)

ENDGAME **80**

W: Kg1, Pf4, Ph4 B: Kf5
White moves and wins

Split-Pawn Defense

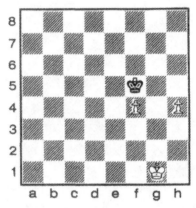

Split pawns, separated by one file, defend each other if they occupy the same rank. When one is attacked, the other advances. If the back one is captured, the pawn in front moves up the board unchecked, too fast to be caught from behind.

1.	h5	Kf6
2.	Kg2	Kg7
3.	f5	Kh6
4.	f6	Kh7
5.	Kg3	Kg8
6.	h6	Kf7
7.	h7	Kxf6
8.	h8/Q+	
	(1–0)	

ENDGAME **81**

W: Kh1, Pa4, Pc5 B: Kb7
White moves and wins

Alignment

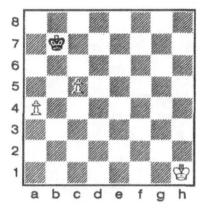

Once the pawns are aligned on the same rank they are un-
assailable if Black does not already attack either of them. Then,
after Black's King threatens one of them, the other is advanced.
While Black tries to hold the fort, White quietly hauls up his
King to join the action. Depending on how Black chooses to
defend, White has several ways to score the point.

1.	a5	Kc6
2.	a6	Kc7
3.	Kg2	Kc6
4.	Kf3	Kc7
5.	Ke4	Kc6
6.	Kd4	Kc7
7.	Kd5	Kc8
8.	c6	Kb8
9.	Kc5	Ka8
10.	c7	Ka7
11.	c8/R	Kxa6
12.	Rc7	Ka5
13.	Ra7	mate

(1–0)

ENDGAME 82

W: Kd4 B: Kc7, Pb5, Pd5
White moves and wins

Opposition

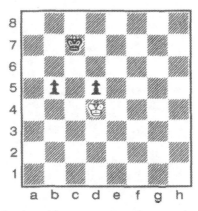

An exception. Isolated pawns—standing on the same rank, one file apart—do not necessarily defend themselves if the enemy King is aggressively posted, possessing the move and already attacking one of the pawns. Yet White cannot just swim home. Taking the d-pawn loses: 1. Kxd5 Kb6 2. Kd4 Ka5 3. Kc3 Ka4 4. Kb2 Kb4 5. Ka2 Kc3, and Black's King has reached a critical square, ensuring his win. Correct is 1. **Kc5**, slipping between the pawns to seize the direct vertical opposition. White follows by capturing the pawn on the file Black's King moves to. If 1. . . . Kd7, for example, White draws by 2. Kxd5 Kc7 3. Kc5 Kb7 4. Kxb5, and Black loses both his pawns.

1.	Kc5	b4
2.	Kxb4	Kd6
3.	Kc3	Ke5
4.	Kd3	d4
5.	Kd2	Ke4

6.	Ke2	d3 +
7.	Kd2	Kd4
8.	Kd1	Kc3
9.	Kc1	d2 +
10.	Kd1	Kd3

Stalemate

W: Kh3 **B:** Kd4, Pf2, Ph4
White moves and draws

Getting Back

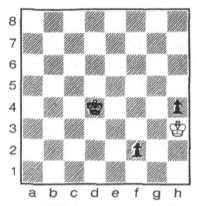

White can draw, but not by a blundering capture of the h-pawn, which allows Black a promotion at f1. Rather, White retreats his King to g2, threatening the f-pawn. After Black defends the pawn, White blockades it: 1. . . . Ke3 2. Kf1. Black then has the unenviable choice of two stalemates: 2. . . . Kf3 or 2. . . . h3.

1. **Kg2** **Ke3**
2. **Kf1** **Kf3**
Stalemate

ENDGAME **84**

W: Kh1, Pb4, Pe4 **B:** Ke5
White moves and wins

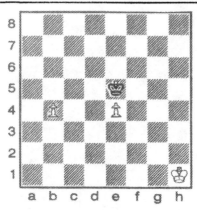

Split pawns separated by two files generally win. If both pawns manage to cross safely over the middle of the board onto the 5th rank, the distance between the pawns (three squares) is no greater than the distance to the Queening square (also three squares). In that case the pawns are self-sustaining, and one or the other Queens by force. Generally, as one pawn is attacked, it is used as a decoy, allowing the second pawn to advance. Black's King is unable to defend two distant points simultaneously. If necessary, White's King can then arrive in time to save the remaining pawn and escort it home. In this instance, however, the pawns are yet to cross the frontier line and the e-pawn faces imminent capture. White can still safeguard his e-pawn by pushing the b-pawn, however, for the capture at e4 pulls Black's King out of the "square of the b-pawn," which then Queens. Thus, instead of capturing the e-pawn, Black's King must retreat to overtake the decoy b-pawn, which then falls. But while Black circles in to capture, White has just enough time to bring up his King and reach a critical square in front of his e-pawn.

1. b5	Kd6	5. Ke5	Kc6	9. e6+	Kd6
2. Kg2	Kc5	6. Ke6	Kc7	10. e7	Ke5
3. Kf3	Kxb5	7. e5	Kd8	11. e8/Q+	
4. Kf4	Kc5	8. Kf7	Kd7	(1–0)	

ENDGAME 85

W: Kg3 B: Kh8, Pe5, Ph5
White moves and draws

Inside the Pawn's Square

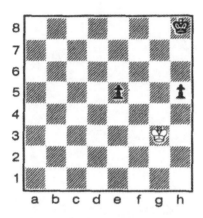

The exception to split pawns generally winning is when one of them is a Rook-pawn. Without the aid of Black's King, his split pawns, two files apart, cannot defend themselves. Black must sacrifice his decoy, the good e-pawn, in order to save the bad h-pawn. Even though Black's King comes forward, it lacks space to maneuver. There simply are no squares to the right of the h-file. The game is drawn, for Black's King will never be able to occupy the h-pawn's critical square, g2.

1.	Kh4	e4
2.	Kg3	Kg7
3.	Kf4	Kg6
4.	Kxe4	Kg5
5.	Kf3	h4
6.	Kg2	Kg4
7.	Kh2	h3
8.	Kh1	Kg3
9.	Kg1	h2 +
10.	Kh1	Kh3

Stalemate

7

King and Pawn vs. King and Pawn

ENDGAME 86

W: Kh2, Pb5 B: Ka8, Pb6
White moves and wins

Outflanking

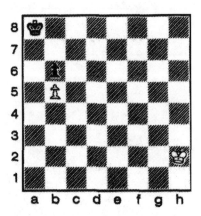

When both sides have a pawn that blocks the other pawn from moving, they are fixed. In fixed-pawn situations, sometimes a King can outmaneuver the other and win the enemy pawn. The technique is known as "outflanking." Fixed pawns have their own critical squares. Each pawn has up to three critical squares to the right of itself along the rank it occupies, and up to three critical squares to the left on the same rank. Thus a fixed pawn in the center could have as many as six critical squares. If the King can occupy any of the enemy fixed pawn's critical squares, it can win the pawn by force, even if the other side's King is momentarily guarding it. The b6-pawn's critical squares are c6, d6, and e6. To win Black's b-pawn, White's King needs merely get to the square e6 to outflank Black's King.

1. Kg3	Kb7	7. Kd7	Kb8	13. b7	Kc7
2. Kf4	Kc7	8. Kc6	Ka7	14. Ka7	Kc6
3. Ke5	Kd7	9. Kc7	Ka8	15. b8/Q	
4. Kd5	Kc7	10. Kxb6	Kb8	(1–0)	
5. Ke6	Kc8	11. Ka6	Ka8		
6. Kd6	Kb7	12. b6	Kb8		

ENDGAME **87**

W: Kc7, Pe5 B: Kg4, Pe6
White moves and wins

Trebuchet

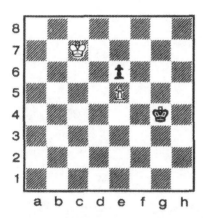

Both Kings have to get closer to the pawns on the e-file, but the pathway to the prey is trecherous. *Zugzwang* positions, where the compulsion to move courts fatality, abound. If, for example, White tries the direct approach, 1. Kd6, Black responds 1. ... Kf5, setting up a *zugzwang* situation known as the "trebuchet. White's King must back off, abandoning his pawn to capture. The correct method for White is to steal up on Black's pawn by 1. **Kd7**, eliciting the reply, 1. ... **Kf5**. Only then does White play 2. **Kd6**, setting up a favorable trebuchet for himself. Now, it is Black's King who must withdraw, allowing White to capture on e6 with an easy win. Observe the characteristic position of the Kings in a trebuchet, a Knight's distance from each other.

1. Kd7	Kf5		5. e6+	Kf8
2. Kd6	Kg6		6. e7+	Kf7
3. Kxe6	Kg7		7. e8/Q+	
4. Kd7	Kf7		(1–0)	

ENDGAME **88**

W: Ka8, Pe5 B: Kf7, Pe6
White moves and wins

Outflanking Trebuchet

The nearest critical squares for White's King to win Black's pawn are b6, c6, and d6, and the closest for Black's King to win White's pawn are f5, g5, and h5. Even though Black's King stands on the file right next to the e-pawns, it is White's King who first reaches one of the critical squares. This feature decides the outcome. If Black chooses to defend passively, White gains the opposition on the 7th rank, exercises a turning or outflanking maneuver on the squares d6 and d7, and picks up the e6-pawn. Should Black try a counterattack against White's e5-pawn, then the same squares—d6 and d7—allow White to execute a winning trebuchet.

	A	
1.	Kb7	Ke7
2.	Kc7	Ke8
3.	Kd6	Kf7
4.	Kd7	Kf8
5.	Kxe6	Ke8
6.	Kf6	Kf8
7.	e6	Ke8
8.	e7	Kd7
9.	Kf7	Kd6
10.	e8/Q	
	(1–0)	

	B	
1.	Kb7	Kg6
2.	Kc6	Kg5
3.	Kd7	Kf5
4.	Kd6	Kg6
5.	Kxe6	Kg7
6.	Kd7	Kf7
7.	e6+	Kf6
8.	e7	Ke5
9.	e8/Q+	
	(1–0)	

ENDGAME **89**

W: Kg1, Pf3 **B:** Kd4, Pf5
White moves and draws

Defensive Pitch

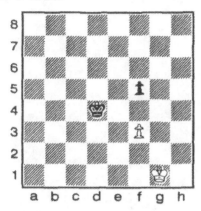

It's crucial that your fixed pawn be on the proper rank when you get outflanked. If it's your 3rd rank, you lose; if it's your 4th rank, you draw. After 1. Kf2 f4, Black outflanks and wins White's pawn on f3, which then becomes a critical square for Black's passed pawn at f4. The pawn then Queens. After 1. f4, Black again wins White's pawn, but then Black's King does not occupy a critical square for his pawn on f5 (its critical squares are e3, f3, and g3). The game is drawn.

1. f4	Ke4
2. Kg2	Kxf4
3. Kf2	Ke4
4. Ke2	f4
5. Kf2	f3
6. Kf1	Ke3
7. Ke1	f2+
8. Kf1	Kf3
	Stalemate

ENDGAME **90**

W: Kb8, Ph2 B: Kb6, Ph3
White moves and draws

Critical Retreating Diagonal

White's King has to move one of two ways. White can move it apparently closer to the pawns, 1. Kc8, and lose (1. . . . Kc6 2. Kd8 Kd5 3. Kc7 Ke4 4. Kd6 Kf3 5.Ke5 Kg2 6. Kf4 Kxh2 7. Kf3 Kg1 8. Kg3 h2, Queening). Or he can move to what seems farther away, 1. Ka8!, and draw, as in the main variation. The twist is that by playing to a8, White's King actually is moving closer to the "critical retreating diagonal," a7-g1, channeling him back to f2 and trapping Black's King after he captures on h2.

	1.	Ka8	Kc6
	2.	Ka7	Kd5
	3.	Kb6	Ke4
	4.	Kc5	Kf3
	5.	Kd4	Kg2
	6.	Ke3	Kxh2
	7.	Kf2	Kh1
	8.	Kg3	h2
	9.	Kf2	
		Stalemate	

ENDGAME **91**

W: Ke6, Pa6 B: Kc3, Pa7
White moves and wins

Shielding Off

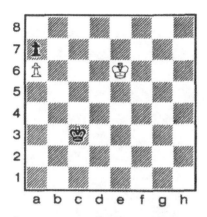

White's monarch can proceed toward Black's pawn at a7, in the same number of moves, with three different first moves: Kd7, Kd6, or Kd5. Only 1. **Kd5**, however, prevents Black's King from maneuvering to the critical diagonal of retreat (h2-b8) to connect to c7, which encloses White's King at a7. The inexact play 1. Kd6?, for example, draws after 1. . . .Kd4 2. Kc6 Ke5 3. Kb7 Kd6 4. Kxa7 Kc7 5. Ka8 Kb6 6. a7 Kc7 stalemate. Thus, when approaching an area or particular square with your King, try to find moves that also hamper the movement of the enemy King.

1. **Kd5** **Kb4**
2. **Kc6** **Ka5**
3. **Kb7** **Kb5**
4. **Kxa7** **Kc6**
5. **Kb8** **Kb6**
6. **a7**

(1–0)

ENDGAME 92

W: Kd6, Pb5 **B:** Ka8, Pa7
White moves and wins

Squeeze

After 1. **Kc7** Black's King is locked in with no way out. This stalemating of his King forces Black to play a losing pawn move. White's pawn is then free to whisk in for the kill, supported all the way by his own king. Black to move draws easily by either Kb7 or Kb8—anything to keep White's King out of the omnipotent c7 square. This position is a kind of squeeze, for White's first move forces Black to impair his position and lose. You are "squeezed" when any move you make worsens your game.

1.	Kc7	a5
2.	b6	a4
3.	b7+	Ka7
4.	b8/Q+	Ka6
5.	Qb6 mate	

(1–0)

ENDGAME **93**

W: Kh2, Pe4 B: Kg4, Pf6
White moves and draws

Changing the Critical Squares

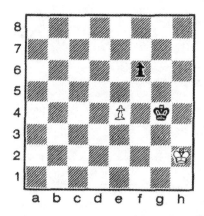

Starting his campaign with a King move yields nothing for White: 1. Kg2 Kf4   2. Kf2 Kxe4, and Black wins because his King sits on a critical square for the f6 pawn. White reasons that since the e-pawn can't be saved, its loss must nevertheless encompass a gain. White pushes his pawn to e5. Black's pawn is forced to capture and winds up one rank farther up the board. This means the critical squares of Black's pawn have also moved up the board, becoming d3, e3, and f3. Since White's King is now closer to the new critical squares, it can prevent Black's King from occupying them.

1.	e5	fxe5
2.	Kg2	Kf4
3.	Kf2	e4
4.	Ke2	e3
5.	Ke1	Kf3
6.	Kf1	e2 +
7.	Ke1	Ke3
	Stalemate	

ENDGAME 94

W: Ka1, Pd4 B: Kb5, Pc6
White moves and draws

Distant Opposition

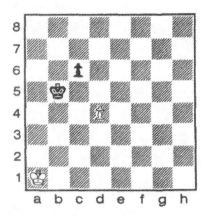

The King will achieve zero by moving directly with 1. Kb1 Kc4 2. Kc2 Kxd4, and Black triumphs simply by occupying a critical square for the c6 pawn. Instead, White musters a twofold defense that works. First, he brings the critical squares closer to his King by sacrificing his own pawn, forcing Black's pawn to capture on d5. Second, after abandoning his pawn, he moves his King, not to b2 (which loses to Black's Kb4), but to b1, to take the distant vertical opposition.

1.	d5	cxd5
2.	Kb1	Kc5
3.	Kc1	Kc4
4.	Kc2	d4
5.	Kd2	d3
6.	Kd1	Kc3
7.	Kc1	d2 +
8.	Kd1	Kd3
	Stalemate	

ENDGAME **95**

W: Kc2, Pb2 B: Kf6, Pa4
White moves and wins

Underpass

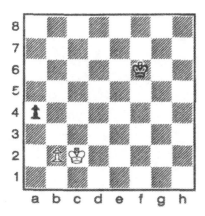

To win, White's King must not only capture the a-pawn, it also must reach a critical square after capturing it in front of the b-pawn. Direct assault by 1. Kc3 fails. Black responds 1. . . . a3!, and if White captures, he is left with an unwinnable a-pawn. Nor does it help after 1. Kc3? a3! to push the b-pawn: (A) 2. b3 Ke5 3. Kc2 Kd4 4. Kb1 Kc3 5. Ka2 Kb4; or (B) 2. b4 Ke5 3. Kb3 Kd5 4. Kxa3 Kc6 5. Ka4 Kb6. The only viable way to demolish the a-pawn is for White's King to cut back and south of his own b-pawn: 1. Kb1!. Now 1. . . . a3 can be answered by 2. b3! (not to b4, transforming into variation B above). And after 2. . . . Ke5 3. Ka2 Kd5 4. Kxa3 Kc5 5. Ka4 Kb6 6. Kb4, White gains the opposition on the 4th rank in front of his b-pawn, ensuring his reaching one of the critical squares on the 5th rank via a turning maneuver.

1.	Kb1	a3
2.	b3	Ke5

3.	Ka2	Kd5
4.	Kxa3	Kc5
5.	Ka4	Kb6
6.	Kb4	Ka6
7.	Kc5	Kb7
8.	Kb5	Ka7
9.	Kc6	Kb8
10.	b4	Ka7
11.	b5	Kb8
12.	Kb6	Ka8
13.	Kc7	Ka7
14.	b6+	Ka8
15.	b7+	Ka7
16.	b8/Q+	Ka6
17.	Qb6	mate

(1–0)

ENDGAME **96**

W: Kb4, Pb6 **B:** Kd7, Pc6
White moves and wins

Squeezing In

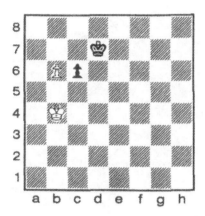

White triumphs directly with 1. **Kc5**, and whether Black retreats his King to c8 or d8 doesn't matter. On 1. . . . Kc8, White captures the c-pawn and nudges Black from the back rank in a squeeze: 2. Kxc6 Kb8 3. b7 Ka7 4. Kc7 Ka6 5. b8/Q Ka5 6. Qb3 Ka6 7. Qb6 mate. After the alternative 1. . . . **Kd8**, White postpones capturing the c-pawn in favor of 2. **Kd6**, opposing Black's King and threatening advance of the b-pawn. To stop this, Black must continue 2. . . . **Kc8**, after which White's King takes the pawn on c6, changing it into the initial winning lines.

1.	Kc5	Kd8
2.	Kd6	Kc8
3.	Kxc6	Kb8
4.	b7	Ka7
5.	Kc7	Ka6
6.	b8/Q	Ka5
7.	Qb3	Ka6
8.	Qb6	mate

(1–0)

ENDGAME 97

W: Kd1, Ph2 B: Kc3, Pf6
White moves and wins

Diagonal Block

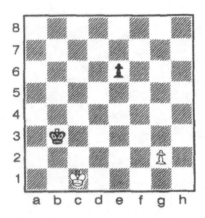

Can White's pawn win the race to Queen? After 1. **h4**, Black's King is within the "square of White's pawn" (an imaginary box extending from h4 to h8 to d8 to d4 when the pawn is on h4), but the critical retreating diagonal leading to the promotion square is blocked by Black's own pawn at f6. Remove that pawn, and Black's King makes it back in time to overtake White's pawn.

1. h4   Kd4
2. h5   Ke5
3. h6   Kf5
4. h7   Kg6
5. h8/Q

(1–0)

ENDGAME 98

W: Kh2, Pa7 B: Kd3, Pf2
White moves and wins

The Skewer

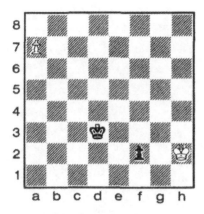

Even if both the Black and White pawns make it to Queensland, the first to edge in the new ladyship gets to give the first check. What follows could lead to mate or winning the other side's Queen through an x-ray attack, or skewer—attacking the enemy King, forcing it to move out of check, and picking up the Queen behind.

1. a8/Q   f1/Q
2. Qa6+ Kd2
3. Qxf1
    (1–0)

ENDGAME 99

W: Kd8, Pa4 B: Kb4, Pf6
White moves and draws

The Feint

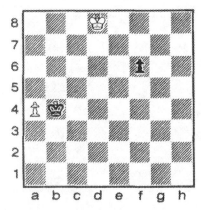

White's King seems ineffectual. It appears it is too far behind Black's f-pawn to overtake it, and too far from his own a-pawn to defend it. If White brings his King back along a stellar diagonal pathway, however, he can retain the possibility of doing either, forcing Black to commit himself. In other words, he is feinting a defense of his a-pawn. Faking movement of your King in one direction so that you gain time to switch to another direction is called a "feint." If Black chooses to make a new Queen, White's King arrives in time to save his a-pawn and make a Queen himself. And if Black's King spends a tempo capturing the a-pawn, White's King can flag down the f-pawn.

	A			**B**	
1.	Kc7	f5	1.	Kc7	f5
2.	Kb6	f4	2.	Kb6	Kxa4
3.	a5	f3	3.	Kc5	f4
4.	a6	f2	4.	Kd4	f3
5.	a7	f1/Q	5.	Ke3	f2
6.	a8/Q		6.	Kxf2	
	Draw			Draw	

ENDGAME **100**

W: Kh8, Pc6 B: Ka6, Ph5
White moves and draws

Diagonal March

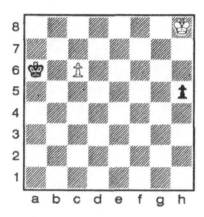

This is Richard Reti's memorable diagonal-march composition. White's King, as in the previous endgame, is hopelessly palled at catching the h-pawn or safeguarding White's own c-pawn before Black's King gets to it. The crux of the problem is to travel the a1-h8 superdiagonal. This endows White's King with the potential of pursuing either a defensive or an aggressive plan. Once Black commits himself, White chooses the other route and draws.

A		**B**	
1. Kg7	h4	1. Kg7	Kb6
2. Kf6	h3	2. Kf6	h4
3. Ke6	h2	3. Ke5	h3
4. c7	h1/Q	4. Kd6	h2
5. c8/Q		5. c7	h1/Q
		6. c8/Q	
Draw		Draw	

8

King and Two Pawns vs. King and Pawn

ENDGAME **101**

W: Kf5, Pe6 **B:** Kg7, Pd6, Pf6
White moves and draws

Clearance

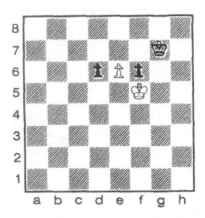

Black's extra pawn confers obtrusive advantage, and if allowed to play 1. . . .d5, he wins comfortably. White's natural try is 1. Ke4, but after 1. . . .Kf8   2. Kd4 Ke7 (2. . . .f5 is also good)   3. Kd5 f5, he loses both e-pawn and the game. White must strike immediately to derive benefit from his aggressively placed King. The solution? He can dump his e-pawn to push Black's King out of the picture. Therefore, 1. **e7 Kf7**   2. **e8/Q + Kxe8.** Now White must tread carefully, as 3. Kxf6? Kd7   4. Kf5 Kc6   5. Ke4 let's Black's King reach the critical outside square, 5. . . .Kc5. The right way is 3. **Ke6! f5**   4. **Kxf5 Kd7**   5. **Ke4 Kc6** 6. **Kd4,** and White recovers just in time.

1.	e7	Kf7
2.	e8/Q +	Kxe8
3.	Ke6	f5
4.	Kxf5	Kd7
5.	Ke4	Kc6
6.	Kd4	

Draw

ENDGAME **102**

W: Ka5, Pf6 **B:** Kh6, Pb7, Pc6
White moves and draws

Diagonal March

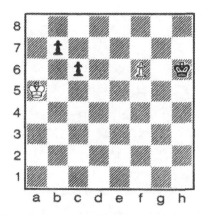

Connected passed pawns possess a ready-made defense when attacked by the King. If the rear pawn is captured, the lead pawn runs for a Queen. Here the presence of the f6-pawn changes the usual setup. White can take with impunity at b7. A diagonal march, feinting at the c-pawn while approaching the f-pawn, prevents a hostile coronation or allows White to coronate too. Either way, White hauls home a draw.

1.	**Kb6**	**Kg6**
2.	**Kxb7**	**c5**
3.	**Kc6**	**c4**
4.	**Kd5**	**c3**
5.	**Ke6**	**c2**
6.	**f7**	**c1/Q**
7.	**f8/Q**	
	Draw	

ENDGAME **103**

W: Kf5, Pe5, Ph5 B: Kf7, Ph6
White moves and wins

Outside Passed Pawn

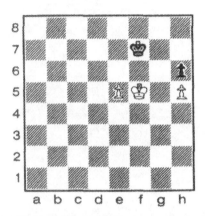

White does not Queen his extra e-pawn, but rather uses it as a decoy to lure Black's King away from the h-pawn. After 1. **e6 +** **Ke7** 2. **Ke5** (a blunder would be 2. Kg6 at once, for 2. . . .Kxe6 3. Kxh6 Kf6 locks up White's King and throws away the key for a draw) **Ke8** 3. **Kf6 Kf8** 4. **Kg6**, White's King captures the defenseless h6-pawn on the next move and occupies g7 a move after that. White's h-pawn then proceeds toward Queendom unmolested.

1.	e6 +	Ke7
2.	Ke5	Ke8
3.	Kf6	Kf8
4.	Kg6	Ke7
5.	Kxh6	Kxe6
6.	Kg7	Kf5
7.	h6	Kg5
8.	h7	Kf5
9.	h8/Q	

(1–0)

ENDGAME **104**

W: Ke6, Pf7, Ph2 **B:** Kf8, Ph7
White moves and wins

Temporizing

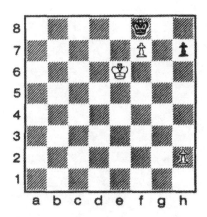

White forcibly stalemates Black's King, 1. **Kf6**, which constrains his opponent to a committal move with his h-pawn: it must play either one or two squares. White then does the opposite of what Black does, and wins. For example, if Black moves his h-pawn one square, White moves his two squares. If Black instead moves his h-pawn two squares, White moves his only one. After this sparring, Back's King is squeezed out.

A		**B**	
1. Kf6	h5	1. Kf6	h6
2. h3	h4	2. h4	h5
3. Kg6	Ke7	3. Kg6	Ke7
4. Kg7	Ke6	4. Kg7	Ke6
5. f8/Q		5. f8/Q	
(1–0)		(1–0)	

ENDGAME **105**

W: Kd5, Pa5, Pc6 B: Kc8, Pa6
White moves and wins

Triangulation

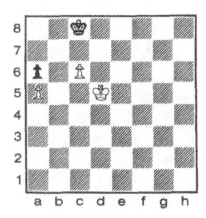

Black to move loses. If 1. . . .Kc7, then White replies 2. Kc5, reaching b6 on the next move and winning the a-pawn. If Black instead tries 1. . . .Kd8 (or 1. . . .Kb8), White squeezes Black out with 2. Kd6 Kc8 3. c7 Kb7 4. Kd7 Ka7 5. Kc6 (delaying the making of a Queen for one move to avoid giving stalemate) Ka8 6. c8/Q+ Ka7 7. Qb7 mate. If White moves first, however, he cannot win with direct entry into Black's position: 1. Kc5 is answered by 1. . . .Kc7, and 1. Kd6 is met by 1. . . .Kd8. The solution is to triangulate White's King (moving it over the squares c4, d4, and d5 to trace an apparent triangle), which breaks the correspondence between the two Kings. It works because White's pawn at c6 restricts Black's maneuvering space, while White's King has the option of moving back to either d4 or c4, both of which pave the way to invasion at c5 or d5, depending on Black's response.

A	
1. Kd4	Kd8
2. Kc4	Kc8
3. Kd5	Kc7
4. Kc5	Kc8
5. Kb6	Kb8
6. Kxa6	Kc7
7. Kb5	Kc8
8. Kb6	Kb8
9. c7+	Kc8
10. a6	Kd7
11. a7	Kc8
12. a8/Q+	Kd7
13. Qe4	Kc8
14. Qe8	mate
(1–0)	

B	
1. Kc4	Kb8
2. Kd4	Kc8
3. Kd5	Kd8
4. Kd6	Kc8
5. c7	Kb7
6. Kd7	Ka7
7. Kc6	Ka8
8. c8/Q+	Ka7
9. Qb7	mate
(1–0)	

ENDGAME 106

W: Kg2, Pf3 B: Kd1, Pe5, Pg5
White moves and draws

Distant Opposition

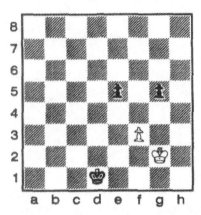

Black to play wins by taking the direct horizontal opposition, 1.
. . .Ke2, and winding around White's King from behind: 2. Kg3
Kf1 3. Kh3 Kf2 4. Kg4 Kg2 5. Kxg5 Kxf3 6. Kf5 e4, and Black
makes a new Queen. If White goes first, he cannot draw by
grabbing the direct horizontal opposition, 1. Kf1, for after a few
King moves, 1. . . .Kd2 2. Kf2 Kd3, it is clear that White's pawn
at f3 is an obstacle, preventing its King from moving to f3 to
maintain direct horizontal opposition. White should start by
securing the distant horizontal opposition, 1. Kh1, after which
the King can freely maneuver to keep the opposition. The only
tactic to worry about after 1. Kh1 is the pawn sacrifice 1. . . .g4,
when Black envisions 2. fxg4 e4 3. g5 e3 4. g6 e2 5. g7 e1/
Q+. But after 1. Kh1 g4, instead of 2. fxg4, White answers 2.
Kg2, when either 2. . . .gxf3+ 3. Kxf3 Kd2 4. Ke4, or 2
. . .Ke2 3. fxg4 e4 4. g5 e3 5. g6 Kd2 6. g7 e2 7. g8/Q e1/
Q will draw.

1. Kh1	Ke1	4. Kh2	Ke3	7. Kxg4	Ke3
2. Kg1	Ke2	5. Kg3	Kd3	8. Kf5	Kxf3
3. Kg2	Kd2	6. Kh3	g5+	9. Kxe5	
					Draw

ENDGAME **107**

W: Ke5, Pf6, Pg5 **B:** Kf8, Pg6
White moves and wins

Pawn Pitch

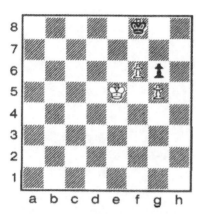

Kingly machinations by White prove nothing: 1. Kd6 Kf7 2. Kd7 Kf8 3. Ke6 Ke8, and Black prevents ingress to this approach. Sometimes an extra f-pawn is too rich for one's game. White doesn't need it. If it weren't there, White's King then has access to the critical outflanking square f6, forcing the gain of Black's g-pawn. The secret to winning an endgame is to give up material advantage for a more advantageous superiority. For example, sacrifice a pawn so that your King can occupy a critical square.

1. f7	Kxf7	7. Kxg6	Kg8
2. Kd6	Kf8	8. Kh6	Kh8
3. Ke6	Kg7	9. g6	Kg8
4. Ke7	Kg8	10. g7	Kf7
5. Kf6	Kh7	11. Kh7	Kf6
6. Kf7	Kh8	12. g8/Q	

(1–0)

ENDGAME **108**

W: Kd4, Pa4, Pb5 **B:** Kc7, Pa5
White moves and wins

Knight's-Move Opposition

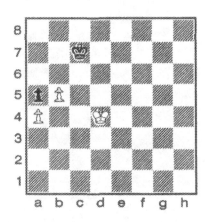

How easy it is to err. After 1. Kc5, taking the direct vertical opposition, White draws quickly if he follows 1. . . .Kb7 with 2. b6?, for 2. . . .Ka6! constrains White to enwrap Black in a stalemate (3. Kc6) or to surrender his b-pawn. By taking the "Knight's-move opposition"—placing the King a Knight's distance away from the enemy King—White cedes the direct vertical opposition to Black when it is undesirable for him to take it. Black could answer 1. **Kd5** with 1. . . .Kd7, but that drops the a5-pawn after 2. Kc5 Kc7 3. b6+ Kb7 4. Kb5. Knight's-move opposition cannot be figured out by any rule. It only applies in positions where both sides have pawns that distort normal oppositional possibilities. It rarely occurs in real games, and when it does, it is determined by a concrete analysis of the position at hand.

1. **Kd5**	**Kb6**	5. **Kb6**	**Kb8**
2. **Kd6**	**Kb7**	6. **Kxa5**	
3. **Kc5**	**Ka7**	(1–0)	
4. **Kc6**	**Ka8**		

W: Kd7, Pb6, Pc5 **B:** Ka8, Pb7
White moves and wins

Pawn Sac

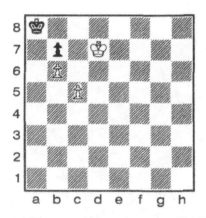

Obtrude White's King onto c7 or c8, and voilà! Stalemate. Black needs the latitude to make legal moves so that his prey can be trapped and set up for mate without the possibility of stalemating him. This is not really hard. After 1. **c6 bxc6** 2. **Kc7**, Black's King is cornered, but his newly created c-pawn is free to move. White is thus granted enough time to promote his pawn and produce mate.

1.	c6	bxc6
2.	Kc7	c5
3.	b7+	Ka7
4.	b8/Q+	Ka6
5.	Qb6	mate

(1–0)

ENDGAME **110**

W: Kd5, Pf5, Pg6 B: Kd7, Pg7
White moves and wins

Breakthrough 1

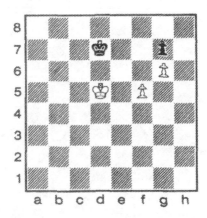

Black's King has wandered too far from the Kingside theater to participate. White juggernauts him with the breakthrough pawn sacrifice 1. f6. However Black retorts, White Queens a pawn a few moves later at g8. The defender in such situations is hampered. In trying to maintain a favorable oppositional relationship with the enemy King, he must also ensure that his own King remains within the "square of a breakthrough pawn" (an imaginary boxed-off block of squares). In order to stay close enough, he eventually may have to surrender the opposition.

A	
1. f6	gxf6
2. g7	Ke7
3. g8/Q	
(1–0)	

B	
1. f6	Ke8
2. fxg7	Ke7
3. g8/Q	
(1–0)	

ENDGAME 111

W: Ke5, Pf5, Pg6 B: Ke7, Pg7
White moves and wins

Outflanking—Opposition

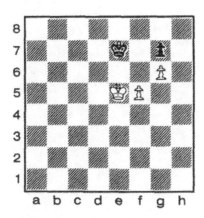

It's White's turn, but Black has the direct vertical opposition. White used Black's tie-up in the Kingside sector to regain the opposition and force entry into Black's territory. After 1. **Kd5**, Black can't follow suit with 1. . . .Kd7 because of 2. f6, a winning breakthrough. So he tries 1. . . . **Kf6**, but after 2. **Ke4 Ke7** 3. **Ke5**, White has stolen the opposition and can outflank: 3. . . . **Ke8** 4. **Ke6 Kf8** 5. **Kd7 Kg8** 6. **Ke7 Kh8**. Now, if White's King comes any closer it will be stalemate, but the advance 7. **f6**, guarantees that Black will possess a pawn free to move, avoiding stalemate, for 7. . . . Kg8 8. f7+ Kh8 9. f8/Q is mate.

1.	Kd5	Kf6	7. f6	gxf6
2.	Ke4	Ke7	8. Kf7	f5
3.	Ke5	Ke8	9. g7+	Kh7
4.	Ke6	Kf8	10. g8/Q+	Kh6
5.	Kd7	Kg8	11. Qg6 mate	
6.	Ke8	Kh8	(1–0)	

ENDGAME **112**

W: Kd5, Pf5, Pg5 B: Kd7, Pg7
White moves and wins

Outflanking 1

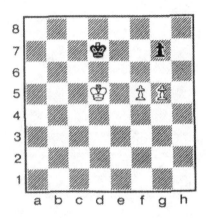

Black has the direct vertical opposition, but White can pinch it away at the right moment by using his reserve tempo, moving the g-pawn. This converts to the winning formations of the previous two endgames, and the same tactics work here.

1.	Ke5	Ke7
2.	g6	Ke8
3.	Ke6	Kf8
4.	Kd7	Kg8
5.	Ke7	Kh8
6.	f6	gxf6
7.	Kf7	f5
8.	g7+	Kh7
9.	g8/Q+	Kh6
10.	Qg6	mate

(1–0)

ENDGAME **113**

W: Ke3, Pg4, Ph2 **B:** Kd5, Pg5
White moves and wins

Corresponding Squares

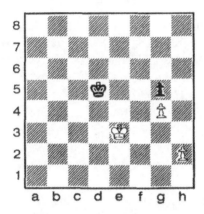

The matter of "corresponding squares" involves only Kings and pawns in the endgame. Corresponding squares determine whether the game can be won. They relate to each other in a certain way. Each King has a square that corresponds to a square important to the other King. In order for one side to win, the enemy King must move to its corresponding square first.

Corresponding squares generally come in sets of two: One for White, and one for Black. These squares usually surface in more complicated endings, in which basic oppositions prognosticate little practical value. Corresponding squares can be determined only by very exact calculation, and there are no simple formulas that can help.

Again, when two squares correspond, it is undesirable for a player to move a King to a corresponding square before his opponent has moved his King to its corresponding square.

Black holds the draw if after White's King moves to a certain square, Black's King can move to one that corresponds. The winning procedure, therefore, is to create multiple invasion threats that force the enemy to commit his King before you do, which allows you to then break the correspondence. The trick in this kind of play is to find out, through calculation and analysis, which squares correspond. There is no other practical way to do it.

In the given position, White wins by getting his King to e4. Then, with Black's King on e6, White uses his reserve tempo (h2-h3), gaining the opposition and outflanking, to filch the g5-pawn. To get to e4, White's King goes to g3, menacing the winning advance h2-h4. Black's King keeps pace within one leftward file of White's. He moves to f6 only after White tries g3. Black meets h2-h4 by trading pawns, followed by Kg6. If Black's King were instead on f7 or g6, White's King wins by reaching e4 (g3-f3-e4). Black, moreover, can safely play Ke5 only after White's Kf3.

Two sets of corresponding squares are salient: g3 for White and f6 for Black is one set; f3 for White and e5 for Black is the other. In other words, White's g3 corresponds to Black's f6, and White's f3 corresponds to Black's e5. Within a set, neither King should move to its corresponding square first. To hold the draw, Black's King shouldn't move to f6 before White's has moved to g3. Black's King can move to either of its two key squares (e5 and f6) only from e6. White has an option. From either f2 or g2, he is able to move to his corresponding squares, f3 or g3. Thus he wavers between f2 and g2, waits for Black to commit himself to f6 or e5, then goes to the matching corresponding square. If Black's King is on f6, White's moves to g3. If it's on e5, White's moves to f3. White's King breaks the correspondence and wins.

1. Kf3	Ke5	8. h3	Kf6
2. Kg3	Kf6	9. Kd5	Kf7
3. Kg2	Ke6	10. Ke5	Kg6
4. Kf2	Kf6	11. Ke6	Kg7
5. Kg3	Kg6	12. Kf5	Kh6
6. Kf3	Kf6	13. Kf6	Kh7
7. Ke4	Ke6	14. Kxg5	

(1–0)

W: Ka1, Pe4 B: Ka8, Pe5, Pf6
White moves and draws

Long-Distant Opposition

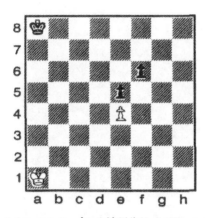

Black has an extra pawn, but if White's King seizes the long-distant opposition, 1. **Ka2**, Black can be prevented from making inroads into White's camp and the game is drawn. After 1. **Ka2**, the Kings stand five squares apart—an odd number—along the direct path of the a-file. The Kings also occupy squares of the same color, which must be, if the Kings stand in true opposition, unaffected by the fixture of pawns. By maintaining the opposition along the entire board, whether the distant or the direct kind, White holds the position together.

1.	Ka2	Ka7	8. Kd3	Ke7
2.	Ka3	Ka6	9. Ke3	Kf7
3.	Ka4	Kb6	10. Kf3	Kg7
4.	Kb4	Kb7	11. Kg3	Kg6
5.	Kb3	Kc6	12. Kg4	Kh6
6.	Kc4	Kc7	13. Kh4	
7.	Kc3	Kd7	Draw	

ENDGAME 115

W: Kh1, Pf4, Pg5 **B:** Kh5, Pf7
White moves and draws

Jettison

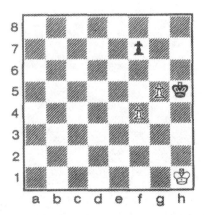

White seems a winner, with an extra pawn in his arsenal. Yet White's two pawns are less than Black's one, for both of White's are lost: 1: Kg1 Kg4 2. Kg2 Kxf4 3. Kf2 Kxg5. Also, Black's King occupies a critical square (g5) for his pawn at f7. Since both pawns will go down anyway, why not shed them so that the critical squares for Black's f-pawn slide farther up the board, making it harder for Black's King to reach them? White draws by sacrificing both pawns, in each case forcing Black's pawn to capture and move up, closer to White's own King. Black's critical squares, once e5, f5, and g5, now become e3, f3, and g3.

1. g6	fxg6	6. Kf2	f3
2. f5	gxf5	7. Kf1	Kg3
3. Kg1	Kg5	8. Kg1	f2+
4. Kf1	Kg4	9. Kf1	Kf3
5. Kg2	f4		Stalemate

ENDGAME **116**

W: Kg4, Pg5, Ph5 B: Ke5, Ph7
White moves and wins

Breakthrough

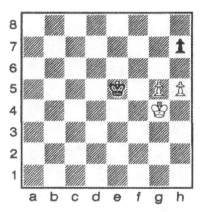

You have a pawn majority when, over any group of consecutive files, your pawns outnumber your opponent's. Capablanca's rules states that you start mobilizing a pawn majority by pushing the unopposed pawn, the one with no enemy pawn ahead of it on the same file. This generally eases the creation of a passed pawn, which is unrestricted by enemy pawns from in front or on the side. But that strategy fails here: 1. g6 hxg6 2. hxg6 Kf6 3. Kh5 Kg7, and the pawn is blockaded; or 1. g6 hxg6 2. h6 Kf6 3. Kh4 Kf7 4. Kg5 Kg8 5. Kxg6 Kh8, with a positional draw. To win, White defies the rule and pushes the opposed pawn instead, 1. h6. After 1. . . .Ke6 2. g6, Black cannot stop White from promoting at h8.

1. h6   Ke6
2. g6   h × g6
3. h7   Kf7
4. h8/Q
(1–0)

ENDGAME **117**

W: Ke3, Pc4, Pd4 B: Ke6, Pc6
White moves and wins

Outflanking

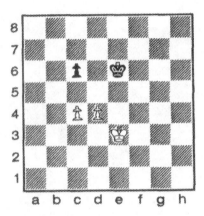

First White's King takes the opposition, then he wades in gradually through a general outflanking until Black's c-pawn is won.
If after 1. **Ke4** Black responds 1. . . .Kf6, then White continues
outflanking to the right with 2. Kf4. But White does not try 2.
d5?, because of 2. . . .Ke7, after which Black is prepared for
several drawing methods. So after 1. . . .Kf6 2. Kf4 Ke6 3.
Kg5 Ke7 4. Kf5 Kd7 5. Ke5, White glides into the main line.

1.	Ke4	Kd6
2.	Kf5	Kd7
3.	Ke5	Ke7
4.	c5	Kd7
5.	Kf6	Kd8
6.	Ke6	Kc7
7.	Ke7	Kc8

8.	Kd6	Kb7
9.	Kd7	Kb8
10.	Kxc6	Kc8
11.	Kb6	Kb8
12.	c6	Kc8
13.	c7	Kd7
14.	Kb7	Kd6
15.	c8/Q	

(1–0)

ENDGAME **118**

W: Kh6, Pg5, Ph2 B: Kg8, Ph7
White moves and wins

Reserve Tempo

White can move his h-pawn either one or two squares, and the right choice is crucial. A move of two squares, 1. h4?, peeters the game to a draw after 1. . . .Kh8   2. h5 Kg8   3. g6 hxg6   4. hxg6 Kh8   5. g7+ Kg8   6. Kg6. A one-square move, however, gains White the opposition later when the g-pawn reaches the 6th rank. If Black's King starts on h8 instead of g8, White then plays his h-pawn two squares to garner the opposition as the pawn later moves to the 6th rank. Think of color to help fix the situation in your mind. If your unmoved pawn is a Rook-pawn, move it to the same color square occupied by the enemy King. If the unmoved pawn is a Knight-pawn, move it to a different color square from that of the enemy King's. Just remember: Rook-pawns play the same, Knight-pawns a different game.

1. h3	Kh8	5. hxg6	Kg8
2. h4	Kg8	6. g7	Kf7
3. h5	Kh8	7. Kh7	Kf6
4. g6	hxg6	8. g8/Q	

(1–0)

9

Miscellaneous King and Pawn Positions

Endgames 119–128

ENDGAME 119

W: Kb6, Pa4, Pc4 **B:** Kb3, Pa5, Pc5
White moves and wins

Direct Opposition

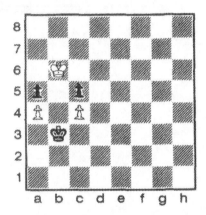

Direct vertical opposition is the cure-all. Instead of exchanging pawns (1. Kxc5 Kxa4 or 1. Kxa5 Kxc4), White wins both of Black's pawns without ceding any of his own. First, the direct opposition is plundered, 1. Kb5!. If Black's King gives way to the a-file, White captures the a-pawn; if Black goes to the c-file, White pilfers the c-pawn. In both cases, White gets something for nothing and shortly promotes a pawn unhindered.

	A			**B**	
1.	Kb5	Ka3	1.	Kb5	Kc3
2.	Kxa5	Kb3	2.	Kxc5	Kb3
3.	Kb5	Kc3	3.	Kb5	Kc3
4.	a5		4.	c5	
	(1–0)			(1–0)	

ENDGAME **120**

W: Ke6, Pf4, Pg3, Ph4 **B:** Kh7, Pf5, Pg6, Ph5
White moves and wins

Horizontal Opposition

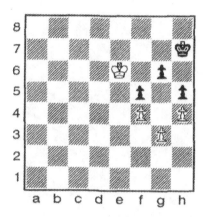

White's assumption of the direct horizontal opposition victimizes Black *tout de suite*. After 1. **Kf7 Kh6** 2. **Kg8!**, Black's King has no moves, so the g-pawn must be advanced and sacrificed, 2. . . . **g5**. Subsequently comes the Queening of White's new g-pawn.

1.	Kf7	Kh6
2.	Kg8	g5
3.	hxg5 +	Kg6
4.	Kh8	Kf7
5.	Kh7	Kf8
6.	g6	Ke7
7.	g7	Kf7
8.	g8/Q +	

(1–0)

ENDGAME **121**

W: Kg8, Pe4, Ph4 B: Kg6, Pe5, Ph6, Ph5
White moves and wins

Rear Outflanking

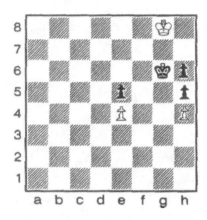

Black has a messy extra pawn, which impedes his King's ability
to retain the direct vertical opposition. Thus, after 1. **Kh8**,
Black's h6-pawn thwarts its King from occupying h6 to maintain
the direct opposition. White wins both Black h-pawns: 1. . . .
Kf6 2. **Kh7 Kf7** 3. **Kxh6 Kf6** 4. **Kxh5**. But the ravaging
doesn't stop there. White also wins the e-pawn: 4. . . . **Kf7** 5.
Kg5 Kg7 6. **Kf5**. From there, who couldn't Queen a pawn?

1.	Kh8	Kf6
2.	Kh7	Kf7
3.	Kxh6	Kf6
4.	Kxh5	Kf7
5.	Kg5	Kg7
6.	Kf5	Kh6
7.	Kxe5	Kh5
8.	Kf6	Kxh4
9.	e5	

(1–0)

ENDGAME **122**

W: Kf5, Pb3, Pc4, Pe6 B: Ke8, Pb4, Pc5, Pc6
White moves and wins

Triangulation

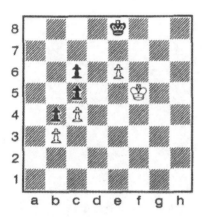

A typical triangulation problem. It's White's move, but to be able to win, White must recreate the same position when it's Black's turn. Black must then make some concession, either allowing White's King to invade at d6 (winning all of Black's pawns), or rewarding White with the opposition, at which point White promotes the e-pawn directly.

1.	Ke4	Kd8
2.	Kf4	Ke8
3.	Kf5	Ke7
4.	Ke5	Ke8
5.	Kd6	Kd8
6.	Kxc6	Ke7
7.	Kd5	Ke8
8.	Kxc5	

(1–0)

ENDGAME 123

W: Kc2, Pb3, f4, g3, h4 B: Ka3, Pa5, f5, g6, h5
White moves and wins

Oppositional Fight

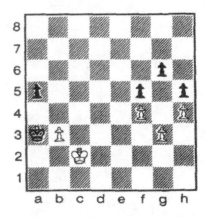

The clue here is that after the exchange of Queenside pawns, Black's King will be one step behind White's in reaching the Kingside theater. Arriving first, White' early-bird monarch gormandizes the g6-pawn, then marks time with the direct vertical opposition. Black's King goes right or left, White's King captures the pawn on the same file as Black's King, and Black realizes nothing in exchange. White is in line for a new Queen.

1.	Kc3	Ka2
2.	b4	axb4
3.	Kxb4	Kb2
4.	Kc4	Kc2
5.	Kd4	Kd2
6.	Ke5	Ke3
7.	Kf6	Kf3
8.	Kxg6	Kxg3
9.	Kg5	

(1–0)

ENDGAME 124

W: Ke5, Pf5, Pg5, Ph5 **B:** Ke7, Pg7, Ph7
White moves and wins

Oppositional Field

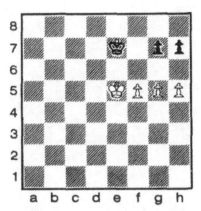

White's double indemnity either locks out Black's King (variation A) or transforms into positions similar to earlier endgames (variation B). Even if Black exchanges pawns, 1. g6 hxg6 2. hxg6, he is left with losing situations essentially like the main variations. In variation A, Black chooses his form of self-execution, allowing the Queening of White's f-pawn or g-pawn. In B, Black gets mated.

	A			B	
1.	g6	h6	1.	g6	h6
2.	Kd5	Kf6	2.	Kd5	Kf6
3.	Ke4	Kg5	3.	Ke4	Ke7
4.	Ke5	Kxh5	4.	Ke5	Ke8
5.	Ke6	Kg5	5.	Ke6	Kf8
6.	f6	Kxg6	6.	Kd7	Kg8
7.	f7	h5	7.	Ke7	Kh8
8.	f8/Q		8.	f6	gxf6
	(1–0)		9.	Kf7	f5
			10.	g7 +	Kh7
			11.	g8/Q mate	
				(1–0)	

ENDGAME **125**

W: Kf1, Pa2, Pd4 B: Kf3, Pe6, Pf7
White moves and wins

Blocking the Critical Diagonal

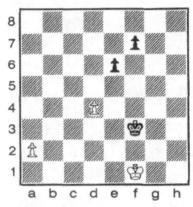

It would take five moves for White to make a new Queen directly by pushing his a-pawn to a8. Black's King gets back also in five moves, retreating along the a8-h1 diagonal—the main strip—and snaps the pawn in time to prevent Queening. Another angle is that after 1. a4, Black's King gets within the "square of White's a-pawn" (the box of squares imagined from a4 to a8 to e8 to e4) by 1. . . . Ke4. A logical solution is to erect a detour, 1. **d5 exd5**, blocking the critical retreating diagonal. Even though Black's King moves inside the "square of the pawn," the d5 roadblock thwarts his timely arrival.

1. d5   exd5
2. a4   d4
3. a5   d3
4. Ke1
(1–0)

ENDGAME **126**

W: Kh1, Pa5, Pb5, Pc5 B: Kh8, Pa7, Pb7, Pc7
White moves and wins

Breakthrough Combination 1

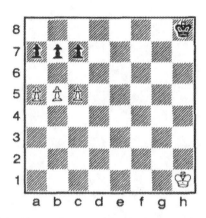

Former World Champion Mikhail Botvinnik once used this position to define "combination," or a forced sequence of moves usually involving sacrifice and leading at least to a positional improvement, if not a win. Some of the early computer programs designed by the brilliant C. E. Shannon in the late '40s even utilized the three pawns vs. three pawns game as a system test to see if things were working properly. Since the Kings are too far away to be involved, the pawns war by themselves. After 1. b6, Black is forced to take White's pawn, else it captures one of his. If Black's a-pawn takes, White lures away the b-pawn and Queens at a8. If Black's c-pawn takes, White deflects the b-pawn toward the a-file, and Queens at c8.

A		**B**	
1. b6	axb6	1. b6	cxb6
2. c6	bxc6	2. a6	bxc6
3. a6	any	3. c6	any
4. a7	any	4. c7	any
5. a8/Q		5. c8/Q	
(1–0)		(1–0)	

ENDGAME **127**

W: Ka1, Pe5, Pf4, Pg4, Ph5 B: Ka3, Pe6, Pf7, Pg7, Ph6
White moves and wins

Breakthrough Combination 2

This problem resembles its immediate predecessor. After 1. f5,
Black loses if he continues 1. . . . exf5, for 2. gxf5 Kb4 3. e6
fxe6 4. fxe6 leads to a new White Queen at e8. Moreover,
1. . . . Kb4 2. g5 exf5 concludes similarly after 3. g6 fxg6 4.
e6. Since the Kings are vacationing from the main action, the
pawns again spit their own fire. Both sides are gifted with
passed pawns, but because White's starts off farther up the
board than Black's, White Queens two moves ahead of his
opponent and wins.

1.	f5	Kb4
2.	g5	hxg5
3.	f6	gxf6
4.	h6	g4
5.	h7	g3
6.	h8/Q	g2
7.	Qg7	

(1–0)

ENDGAME 128

W: Kg2, Pa6, Pc5 B: Kc6, Pc7, Pf4, Pg4, Ph4
White moves and wins

Tempo

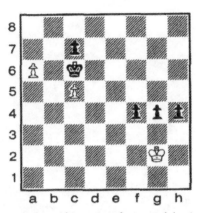

It's not Black's turn, but if it were, he would win by pushing his pawn to g3; however White responds, Black promotes a pawn to Queendom. Note that the Queenside is frozen for both players. If Black were to capture the c-pawn, White's a-pawn would Queen in two moves. If White were to push his pawn to a7, Black's King would get to b7 and overtake it. If White plays first, he wins by 1. **Kg1**, waiting for Black to commit himself. On the Queenside, if Black then moves his King, White's a-pawn Queens. On the Kingside, whichever pawn Black pushes, White's King snuffles into the square immediately in front, stopping the entire three-pawn cluster. After 1. **Kg1**, there follows either: (A) 1. . . . f3 2. Kf2 h3 3. Kg3; (B) 1. . . . h3 2. Kh2 f3 3. Kg3; or (C) 1. . . . g3 2. Kg2; Black has met his Waterloo.

1. **Kg1**	f3	5. **Kg2**	g3
2. **Kf2**	h3	6. **Kh1**	Kxc5
3. **Kg3**	f2	7. **a7**	Kb6
4. **Kxf2**	h2	8. **a8/Q**	

(1–0)

PART

THREE

Pieces and Pawns in Action

In Part Three, the pieces reappear, but in no way diminishing the role of the Kings. Even the Crowned Head is a fighting piece, and in the endgame must be mobilized like the other forces. The dominant issue, however, is still pawn promotion. All the pieces, including Kings, are pressed into service, either supporting or thwarting a Queening operation.

Blocking the path of a passed pawn is a frequent defensive tactic. Doubled and separated pawns invite blockade. Minor pieces (Bishops and Knights) particularly rally to the task, entrenching on the square directly in front of the pawn. In contrast, the major pieces (Queens and Rooks) are misused as blockaders, for their mobility suffers too greatly. Queens and Rooks shine in counterattack rather than in pure defense, harassing the enemy King with incessant checks and threats. Thus emerges a leitmotif for major piece endings: creating shelter for your King against checks.

A passed pawn becomes menacing when a blockade cannot be set up or when the blockading unit is driven from its post. This often happens, for example, by connected, side-by-side pawns that advance in tandem. In such instances, the only way to save the game may be to sacrifice a minor piece for the deadly passed pawn, especially if it is your opponent's last pawn. In that case, his extra Bishop or Knight may be insufficient to force checkmate and the game is drawn.

Pawns near the edge of the board will alter the scenario of many endgames. Generally, the closer the pawns are to the outside, the less the maneuvering room for pieces in attack or defense. Endings with Knight-pawns or Rook-pawns often provide specially favorable or unfavorable exceptions to the rule. Rook-pawns, in particular, have an odious reputation for producing drawn games. When the only pawn on the board is a Bishop-pawn or center-pawn, a Queen or Rook, either in attack or defense, may have great flexibility. But if the lone pawn is on the Knight-file or the Rook-file, the powers of the major pieces are atrophied. They can't function in balance on either side of the pawn (pawns on Rook-files don't have two sides). Of course, the least effective defender against the Rook-pawn is the Knight, which is awkward at best in zeroing in on the corner, and slower than the other pieces in getting back.

10

Heavy Pieces vs. Pawn

ENDGAME **129**

W: Kg8, Qd6 B: Kf2, Pg2
White moves and wins

Blocking the Queening Square

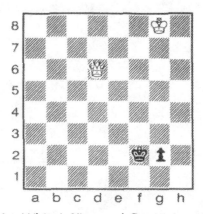

In order to win, White's King and Queen must act as a united force against Black's King and dangerous pawn. But White's King is too far away to help the lady. The winning method is for the Queen to give a series of checks and threats, ultimately forcing Black's King onto the promotion square. This grants White a one-move respite, because Black's pawn can't move with his own King in the way at g1, and White capitalizes by bringing his King one square closer. The process is then repeated, again and again forcing Black's King in front of the pawn, until White's King is close enough to support mate or help win the pawn.

1. Qf4 +	Ke2	7. Kg6	Kf1	13. Qh4 +	Kg1
2. Qg3	Kf1	8. Qf4 +	Ke2	14. Kg4	Kf1
3. Qf3 +	Kg1	9. Qg3	Kf1	15. Qh3	Kf2
4. Kg7	Kh2	10. Qf3 +	Kg1	16. Qf3 +	Kg1
5. Qf2	Kh1	11. Kg5	Kh2	17. Kg3	Kh1
6. Qh4 +	Kg1	12. Qf2	Kh1	18. Qxg2	mate

(1–0)

ENDGAME **130**

W: Kf7, Ph7 B: Kc1, Qd4
White moves and draws

Stalemate 1

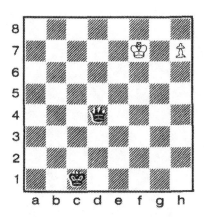

If Black could only move first, he would play his Queen to h8, occupying the promotion square and dousing any real chances for White to convoy his pawn. But White goes first and plays 1. **Kg8**, threatening to make a new Queen. After 1. . . .**Qd8+** 2. **Kg7 Qg5+** 3. **Kf7 Qh6** 4. **Kg8 Qg6+** 5. **Kh8**, Black sees the handwriting on the wall: he can't take advantage of White's pawn being blocked to bring his King closer because it would stalemate White. Normally, a Queen defeats a pawn one square from Queening by forcing the enemy King to occupy the promotion square. But against the Rook-pawn, this strategy succumbs to the threat of stalemate.

1. **Kg8** **Qd8+**
2. **Kg7** **Qg5+**
3. **Kf7** **Qh6**
4. **Kg8** **Qg6+**
5. **Kh8**
   Draw

ENDGAME 131

W: Kd6, Pf7 B: Kb3, Qa1
White moves and draws

Stalemate 2

The general rule states that a Queen will win against a pawn on the 7th rank. The Bishop pawn is an exception, as is the Rook-pawn (illustrated in the previous endgame). Once White's King reaches g8 and meets the anticipated Queen check at g6, it is not obliged to step back into the path of White's pawn at f8. Instead, White may safely abandon the pawn and curl up in the corner. If Black's Queen then captures the pawn at f7, White is stalemated. So Black has no better than a draw.

1.	Ke7	Qe5 +
2.	Kd7	Qf6
3.	Ke8	Qe6 +
4.	Kf8	Kc4
5.	Kg7	Qe7
6.	Kg8	Qg5 +
7.	Kh7	Qf6
8.	Kg8	Qg6 +
9.	Kh8	Qxf7
	Stalemate	

ENDGAME 132

W: Kc2, Qg3 B: Kf1, Pf2
White moves and wins

Mate in Two

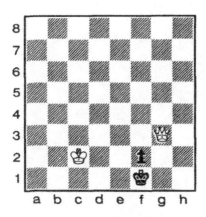

A Bishop pawn on its 7th rank normally draws against a Queen. But the conditions have to be right. First, the defending King must be able to play into the corner (here, h1). Second, the attacking King cannot be nearby. In this endgame, Black's King has no escape to the corner and White's King is at the door, so White wins easily. He can trounce on the f-pawn by 1. Kd3 Ke1 2. Ke3, or he can lob home to mate in two moves by 1. **Qg4 Ke1 2. Qd1.**

1. **Qg4 Ke1**
2. **Qd1 mate**
(1–0)

ENDGAME 133

W: Kg7, Qg8 B: Kh1, Ph2
White moves and wins

Gaining Time

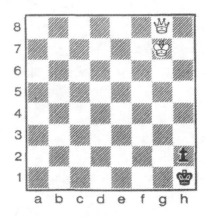

You can defeat a Rook's pawn on the 7th rank by creating a "mate net" with King and Queen. This is done in three stages. First, White's King approaches two squares closer to Black's: 1. **Kg6 Kg2** 2. **Kf5 + Kf2.** Next, the Queen assumes a post on the 2nd rank (Black's 7th rank), level with Black's pawn: 3. **Qd5 Kg1** (Black cannot permit 4. Qh1) 4. **Qd1 + Kg2** 5. **Qe2 + Kg1.** Finally, White's King advances two additional squares, a position that is a Knight's distance from the Queening square (h1): 6. **Kf4 h1/Q** 7. **Kg3.** At this point, Black can delay mate for only a few paltry moves, and only by jettisoning his Queen.

1.	Kg6	Kg2
2.	Kf5 +	Kf2
3.	Qd5	Kg1
4.	Qd1 +	Kg2
5.	Qe2 +	Kg1
6.	Kf4	h1/Q
7.	Kg3	Qd5
8.	Qe1	mate

(1–0)

ENDGAME **134**

W: Kf8, Qg8 B: Ka1, Pa2, Pg4
White moves and wins

No Stalemate

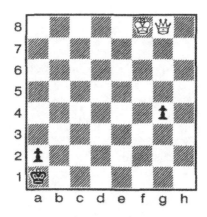

A Rook-pawn on the 7th rank supported by its own King draws against a Queen if the enemy King can't also join in the attack. The usual tactic of forcing the Black King to occupy the square in front of its pawn, so that White's King gains a move to come closer, doesn't work because of stalemate. But here the presence of a second Black pawn on g4 evokes another possibility. It allows White's Queen to trap Black's King for two moves, without fear of stalemate, as White's g-pawn plays to g3 and g2. During the interim, White's Queen slices through to unstoppable mate.

1. **Qb3**   **g3**
2. **Qc2**   **g2**
3. **Qc1**   **mate**
(1–0)

ENDGAME 135

W: Ka8, Rb7 B: Kg6, Ph5
White moves and wins

Cut-Off Along Rank

A Rook's powerful ability to control an entire rank or file means that it can set up impenetrable barriers the enemy King can't cross. Thus it becomes possible to actually shut out Black's King from war games. After 1. **Rb5**, White's Rook establishes a dense force field against Black's King. If Black tries to Queen his pawn without the aid of his King, White's Rook moves in by itself. It waits for the pawn to reach its 6th rank, 1. . . . h4 2. Kb7 h3, then attacks it directly from along the rank, 3. Rb3. The pawn must then advance to avoid capture, 3. . . . h2, and the Rook gets behind it, 4. Rh3, preventing the pawn's promotion and taking it next move. Inevitable doom for Black comes with the arrival of White's King, which wins the pawn, mates, or both.

1.	Rb5	Kh6		7.	Kf6	h3
2.	Kb7	Kg6		8.	Rb3	Kh7
3.	Kc6	Kh6		9.	Rxh3 +	Kg8
4.	Kd6	Kg6		10.	Rh6	Kf8
5.	Ke6	Kh6		11.	Rh8	mate
6.	Kf7	h4			(1–0)	

ENDGAME **136**

W: Kf6, Rg8 B: Kc5, Pb4
White moves and wins

Getting Back

Black's pawn and King are farther advanced than in the previous example, and a Rook cut-off along the rank simply doesn't work. A win hinges on the speediest possible return of White's King. The Rook works from behind, along the ranks; at the proper moment, it checks the enemy King to displace it or to ease the entry of White's King. Generally, the Rook is ideally placed posted behind the pawn, attacking the foot soldier and all the squares the pawn must eventually pass over. Once behind the pawn, the Rook can also shift forward or backward one square, whenever White needs to tempo, without changing the basic situation. In the final position, Black's pawn is lost, and so is his King. After 8. **Kc3**, mate follows regardless of which of Black's four moves are essayed: (A) 8. . . . Kb1 9. Kxb3 Kc1 10. Rd7 Kb1 11. Rd1; (B) 8. . . . Ka1 9. Rxb3 Ka2 10. Kc2 Ka1 11. Ra3; (C) 8. . . . b2 9. Rxb2+ Ka3 10. Rb4 Ka2 11. Kc2 Ka3 12. Rc4 Ka2 13. Ra4; or (D) 8. . . . Ka3 9. Ra7.

1.	**Ke5**	**Kc4**	4.	**Rc8 +**	**Kb2**	7.	**Rb7**	**Ka2**
2.	**Ke4**	**Kc3**	5.	**Kd2**	**Ka2**	8.	**Kc3**	
3.	**Ke3**	**b3**	6.	**Rb8**	**Rk2**		(1–0)	

ENDGAME 137

W: Kc3, Rb8 B: Ka1, Pa2
White moves and wins

Reposition

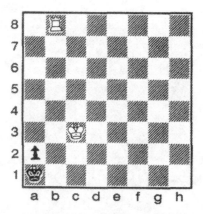

To win, White must tick off two items on his list: first he must realign his King to attack the pawn, and then he must ward off stalemate. Both goals see daylight with 1. **Kb3**, which advances the King toward the pawn and blocks the Rook along the b-file so that Black's King has a safe move, 1. . . . **Kb1**. After 2. **Ka3 +**, Black has to play 2. . . . **Ka1** if he wishes to protect his pawn. But 3. **Rh8** shifts the Rook to the flank, where it can harass Black's King and pick off the luckless footman.

1.	Kb3	Kb1
2.	Ka3 +	Ka1
3.	Rh8	Kb1
4.	Rh1 +	Kc2
5.	Kxa2	

(1–0)

W: Kb7, Rb2 B: Kb5, Pb4
White moves and wins

Tempo Finesse—Opposition

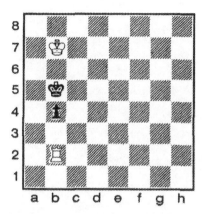

White needs the opposition to force Black's King to commit to one side of the pawn or the other. If Black's King then goes to the a-file, White's King retreats along the c-file, unhampered. If Black's King moves to the c-file, White's King plays back unchecked on the a-file. A tempo move should be played to seize the opposition, and this is achieved by prompting the Rook back to b1. Thereby, the Rook is also farther away from the oncoming Black pawn and King. This makes the Rook safer and more able to wield its own power, for a Rook truly shines as a long-range piece.

1.	**Rb1**	Kc4
2.	**Ka6**	b3
3.	**Ka5**	Kc3
4.	**Ka4**	b2
5.	**Ka3**	Kc2
6.	**Rxb2 +**	

(1–0)

ENDGAME **139**

W: Kf6, Pg6 B: Kb1, Rh5
White moves and wins

Badly Placed Rook

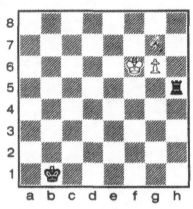

If the powerful Rook is too close to its targets, disaster can ensue. After 1. g7, Black's Rook cannot stop White's pawn from Queening, and merely essays a feeble check, 1. . . .Rh6 +. White eyes with distrust 2. Kf7?, for that allows Black to pin the pawn, 2. . . .Rh7, and to sacrifice the Rook for it the move after. Getting out of check by 2. Ke5 is no better, for Black then wins with 2. . . .Rg6. Nor does 2. Kg5 help any, for Black then hies his Rook to h1, where it can play to g1, skewering White's King and pawn, or King and new Queen. But by moving back along the f-file, 2. Kf5 Rh5 + 3. Kf4 Rh4 + 4. Kf3 Rh3 +, White can play 5. Kg2, nullifying Black's Rook. White then forges a new Queen and triumphs.

1. g7   Rh6 +
2. Kf5   Rh5 +
3. Kf4   Rh4 +
4. Kf3   Rh3 +
5. Kg2

(1–0)

ENDGAME **140**

W: Kb6, Pc6 B: Ka1, Rd5
White moves and wins

Underpromotion

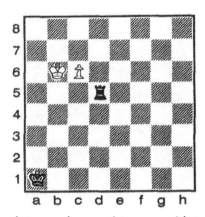

This position relates to the previous one. After 1. **c7**, Black can do nothing but check with his Rook along the ranks, driving White's King back toward Black's. At the first critical juncture, 1. . . .**Rd6+** 2. **Kb5 Rd5+** 3. **Kb4 Rd4+** 4. **Kb3 Rd3+** 5. **Kc2**, Black can no longer give safe checks, but he has the resource: 5. . . .**Rd4!**. Now if White crowns a new Queen, 6. **c8/Q?**, Black plays 6. . . .**Rc4+**, forcing 7. **Qxc4** stalemate. White averts this snare, however, underpromoting to a Rook, 6. **c8/R!**. Now the Rook sacrifice 6. . . .**Rc4+** 7. **Rxc4** does not produce stalemate. Meanwhile, White threatens mate at a8 with his Rook, so Black must continue 6. . . .**Ra4** to shield against the looming check. This fails to the neat double attack, 7. **Kb3**, when Black's Rook is menaced by the enemy King (Kxa4) and mate is promised by White's Rook (Rc1). Black cannot cope with the simultaneous threats.

1.	c7	Rd6+	5. Kc2	Rd4
2.	Kb5	Rd5+	6. c8/R	Ra4
3.	Kb4	Rd4+	7. Kb3	
4.	Kb3	Rd3+	(1–0)	

W: Kh1, Pd6, Pe5 B: Kb3, Rb7
White moves and wins

Connected Pawns on 6th Rank

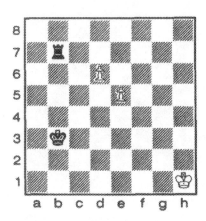

Unless there is a turnabout tactic, connected passed pawns, united on the 6th rank, defeat a Rook if the defending King cannot assist the Rook. After 1. **e6**, White Queens a pawn by force. The skewer 1. . . . .Rb6 attacks both pawns in a line, but White can push either one successfully without really trying.

1. **e6**	**Kc4**
2. **d7**	**Rb8**
3. **e7**	**Kd5**
4. **d8/Q +**	**Rxd8**
5. **exd8/Q +**	
(1–0)	

W: Ka8, Rb7 B: Kh8, Pd3, Pe4
White moves and wins

Rear Attack on Advanced Pawn

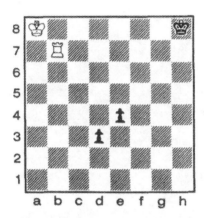

Black has connected passed pawns, but only one has reached the 6th rank while the other is still on the 5th rank. White's Rook might be able to do in the pawns if the enemy King cannot support their advance. The Rook simply attacks the most advanced pawn along the file by going behind it (or, if the situation necessitates, in front). Neither pawn can then budge without the lead pawn being captured for nothing. In the diagram, White plays 1. **Rd7**, and then brings back his King to mop up. Black's King, cut off and out of play, lacks power to do anything.

1.	**Rd7**	**Kg8**
2.	**Kb7**	**Kf8**
3.	**Kc6**	**Ke8**
4.	**Rd4**	**Kf7**
5.	**Kd5**	**e3**
6.	**Rxd3**	**e2**
7.	**Re3**	**e1/Q**
8.	**Rxe1**	

(1–0)

ENDGAME **143**

W: Kg7, Rg2 B: Kb7, Pe3, Pf4
White moves and wins

Frontal Attack

Once again, White's Rook stops both pawns from advancing safely by attacking the lead pawn along the file, this time from in front, 1. **Re2**. White's King then paces back and beats Black's to the pawns, snaring both of them with the aid of the Rook.

1.	**Re2**	Kc6
2.	**Kf6**	Kd5
3.	**Kf5**	f3
4.	**Rxe3**	f2
5.	**Rf3**	f1/Q
6.	**Rxf1**	

(1–0)

ENDGAME **144**

W: Kf6, Rg3 B: Kf8, Pg2, Ph2
White moves and draws

Perpetual Threat

Black has offensive connected pawns on the 7th rank, both ready for Queening in the next move. If the Rook takes the g-pawn, Black's h-pawn takes the honors. The situation looks hopeless, but there's a surprising resource: White threatens mate: 1. **Ra3!**, and Black cannot afford to waste a move pushing either pawn. After Black answers 1. . . .**Kg8**, White starts checking, 2. **Rg3+ Kh7** 3. **Rh3+ Kg8** 4. **Rg3+ Kf8** 5. **Ra3**, and this is where we came in—nothing ventured, nothing gained. So Black flees to the Queenside, 5. . . .**Ke8**, but then White's King joins the drama with mating threats, 6. **Ke6 Kd8** 7. **Kd6 Kc8** 8. **Kc6**. If Black tries 8. . . . .**Kb8**, then White's Rook starts three-ring checking on the Queenside: 9. **Rb3+ Ka7** 10. **Ra3+ Kb8** 11. **Rb3+**. Clearly, Black cannot elude the checks and threats long enough to realize a new Queen. White's perpetual attacks draw the game.

1.	Ra3	Kg8	6.	Ke6	Kd8	11.	Rb3+	Kc8
2.	Rg3+	Kh7	7.	Kd6	Kc8	12.	Ra3	Kd8
3.	Rh3+	Kg8	8.	Kc6	Kb8	13.	Kd6	Ke8
4.	Rg3+	Kf8	9.	Rb3+	Ka7	14.	Ke6	Kf8
5.	Ra3	Ke8	10.	Ra3+	Kb8	15.	Kf6	
							Draw	

11

Minor Pieces vs. Pawn

ENDGAME **145**

W: Kc6, Bd5 B: Ka8, Pa7
White moves and wins

Discovered Mate

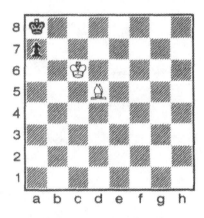

This is paradise for White, Dante's 9th circle for Black. Black's
King is corralled at a8, and his own pawn is an obstacle. White's
King moves up to c7, guarding b8 and unveiling a life-stealing
Bishop. Black is mated.

1. Kc7 mate
(1–0)

ENDGAME 146

Creating a Block

W: Kd5, Pa5, Pg4 B: Kf6, Bh6
White moves and wins

If White rashly advances, 1. a5, Black shifts his Bishop to e3, where it can be sacrificed for the a-pawn if necessary, and the game recedes to a draw. White could retreat his King to e4, to stop the Bishop from going to e3, but it could still play to f8 and then c5, again catching the a-pawn. But White can cross Black with 1. g5+!. If Black's King takes, then the c1-h6 diagonal is blocked and the Bishop can't reach e3 in time to thwart the pawn. If Black instead captures with the Bishop. 1. . . . Bxg5, then White can slant back with his King, 2. Ke4, and the Bishop needs one move more than it did before to reach to f8 and then c5. The a-pawn goes to heaven, gratis.

1.	g5+	Bxg5
2.	Ke4	Bh6
3.	a6	Bf8
4.	a7	Any
5.	a8/Q	

(1–0)

ENDGAME **147**

Pawn's Way

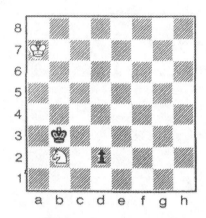

Against an enemy King and any pawn not on a Rook-file, an unassisted Knight can ward off the pawn if the Knight occupies any square in the pawn's path, even a pawn advanced as far as the 7th rank. When the enemy King attacks the Knight from flankside, the steed simply dressages to the other. If the enemy King tries to maneuver to the other wing, White's King strides back just for good measure and enforces the draw.

1.	Nd1	Kc2
2.	Nf2	Kc3
3.	Kb6	Kd4
4.	Kb5	Ke3
5.	Nd1 +	Kd3
6.	Kb4	Kc2
7.	Nf2	Kb1
8.	Kb3	Kc1
9.	Kc3	d1/Q
10.	Nxd1	Kxd1

Draw

ENDGAME 148

W: Kg3, Ne6 B: Kg1, Pf2
White moves and wins

Perpetual Check

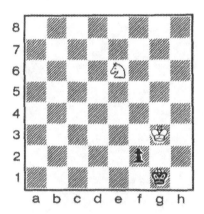

Is White's position hopeless? Black verges on making a new Queen, and neither White's King nor Knight appears powered to stop it. But after **1. Nf4** (not 1. Nd4 f1/Q 2. Nf3 + Kh1, and Black wins) **f1/Q 2. Nh3 + Kh1 3. Nf2 + Kh1 4. Nh3 +**, the only way Black can end the incessant checking is to toss away his lady. This draws, for both sides are left without a shred of material.

1.	Ng4	f1/Q
2.	Nh3 +	Kh1
3.	Nf2 +	Kg1
4.	Nh3 +	Kh1
5.	Nf2 +	Kg1
6.	Nh3 +	
	Draw	

ENDGAME 149

W: Kh1, Nf3 B: Kb3, Pb2
White moves and draws

Knight Fork

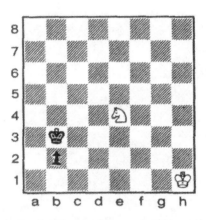

White could go very wrong here, playing 1.Nd4 + ?, when 1.
. . .Kc3 ensures the pawn's safe promotion. The horse move 1.
Nd2 + !, however, wins plaudits, for 1. . . .Kc2 2. Nc4! holds.
After 2. . . .b1/Q, White picks off the newly tiara-ed Queen
with the fork 3. Na3 + . If the Knight cannot occupy a square in
the pawn's path, a draw can still be achieved if the pawn can be
attacked so that if it promotes to a Queen, it can be won with a
forking check.

1.	Nd2 +	Kc2
2.	Nc4	b1/Q
3.	Na3 +	Kc1
4.	Nxb1	Kxb1

Draw

ENDGAME **150**

W: Kb8, Pb6 B: Kh4, Nf6
White moves and wins

The Board's Edge

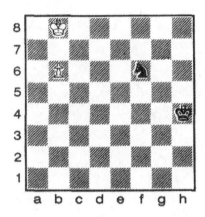

No matter how it's cut, this nugget wins for White after **1. b7**. In variation (A), Black's Knight runs out of room after **1. ...Nd7+ 2. Kc8 Nb6+ 3. Kd8**, when it can't shift to a safe square to guard b8 and stop the pawn. Move the whole scene one file to the right (White King on e8, White pawn on c7, Black Knight on c6), and Black could then jump his Knight to a7, controlling the Queening square and drawing. Thus Knight-pawns present problems for Knights because operations are restricted near the edge.

A		**B**		**C**	
1. **b7**	**Nd7+**	1. **b7**	**Nd5**	1. **b7**	**Ne4**
2. **Kc8**	**Nb6+**	2. **Kc8**	**Ne7+**	2. **Ka8**	
3. **Kd8**		3. **Kd7**			
(1–0)		(1–0)		(1–0)	

ENDGAME 151

W: Kh7, Na3 B: Ke4, Pa2
White moves and draws

Setting the Barrier

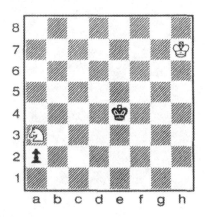

White's first move is a forced 1. **Nc2** to stop the pawn from Queening. At c2, the Knight moreover constructs an impenetrable barrier on the d-file to Black's King. Moving Black's King to d4 is illegal, and moving it to d3 or d5 runs into a forking Knight-check at b4. So the King has to detour (Ke4-f3-e2-d2) to get to the Knight safely. After 1. . . .**Kf3** 2. **Kg6 Ke2** 3. **Kf5 Kd2**, the Knight must retreat to the corner, 4. **Na1**. Meanwhile, as Black's King pursues the Knight, White's King enters the picture steadily: 4. . . . .**Kc1** 5. **Ke4 Kb2** 6. **Kd3**. The finale 6.. . . .**Kxa1** 7. **Kc2** is stalemate, as brought on by the barrier established by the Knight on the first move. It slowed Black's King just enough so that White's King could bring relief for the Knight.

1.	Nc2	Kf3	5.	Ke4	Kb2
2.	Kg6	Ke2	6.	Kd3	Kxa1
3.	Kf5	Kd2	7.	Kc2	
4.	Na1	Kc1		Stalemate	

ENDGAME 152

W: Kh7, Nd4 **B:** Ke3, Pa2
White moves and draws

Setting the Barrier 2

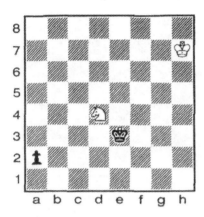

A lone Knight is a mere shadow play against a Rook-pawn on the 7th rank. It needs solid help from its King, else it will end in the corner. So on 1. Nc2+, Black would win by 1. . . .Kd2 2. Na1 Kc1   3. Kg6 Kb2   4. Kf5 Kxa1, and the Knight goes down. The Knight could perhaps buy time for its King to get back with some ammunition. The positioning 1. Nb3 raises a barrier to Black's King on the approachable squares d4, d3, d2, and e2, thanks to the Knight's defensive check at c1. Black's King now must attack over a longer route to get rid of the defending Knight. The extra moves grant White's King time to arrive at c2, to stalemate Black's King after it captures the Knight at a1.

	A		**B**	
1.	Nb3	Ke4	Nb3	Kf2
2.	Kg6	Kd5	Kg6	Ke1
3.	Kf5	Kc4	Kf5	Kd1
4.	Na1	Kc3	Ke4	Kc2
5.	Ke4	Kb2	Na1+	Kb2
6.	Kd3	Kxa1	Kd3	Kxa1
7.	Kc2		Kc2	
	Stalemate		Stalemate	

ENDGAME **153**

W: Ka6, Ng4 B: Kg3, Ph3
White moves and draws

The Circuit

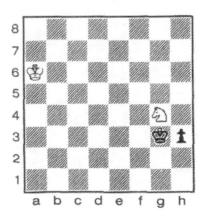

The most difficult pawn for a Knight to meet head on is the Rook-pawn. The Knight can do it if (A) the pawn has not yet reached the 7th rank, and (B) the Knight can control a square in the path of the pawn to the Queening square (though not that square itself). The Knight would naturally be sacrificed to eliminate the dangerous pawn: 1. Ne3 h2 2. Nf1 + Kg2 3. Nxh2. If instead Black's King gives chase, trying to shoo away the Knight, the steed has just enough room to step around the quadrant g4-e3-f1-h2, known as the circuit.

1.	Ne3	Kf3
2.	Nf1	Kf2
3.	Nh2	Kg2
4.	Ng4	Kg3
	Draw	

ENDGAME **154**

W: Kc2, Ne2 **B:** Ka1, Pa3
White moves and wins

Mate in the Corner

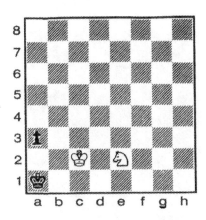

King and Knight cannot mate a lone enemy King. As a team they are not sufficiently powerful. But give Black a far advanced Rook-pawn and confine him to that corner, and suddenly a mating net reticulates. White's first move, 1. Nc1, stalemates Black's King, but Black can still move his a-pawn, 1. . . .a2. At a2, however, the pawn seals off the last escape square and 2. Nb3 is mate.

1. Nc1 a2
2. Nb3 mate
(1–0)

W: Kh2, Pa5 **B:** Kd8, Nb7
White moves and wins

The Dangerous Rook-Pawn

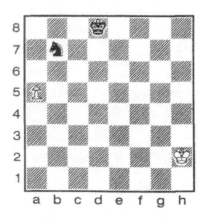

Containing a Rook-pawn's advance is a real thorn in the side of the Knight. The scanty maneuvering room at the edge of the board creates a canyon-size handicap. Here the Knight cannot take up a position to switch to a square in the pawn's path. After 1. **a6**, Black's only hope is 1. . . .**Kc7**, when 2. axb7+? draws to 2. . . .K×b7. Instead, White sends the a-pawn home to Queen.

1. **a6   Kc7**
2. **a7   Nd6**
3. **a8/Q**
    (1–0)

ENDGAME 156

W: Kg3, Ng4, Nh2 B: Kh1, Ph3
White moves and wins

Mate in Two Moves

An extra pawn on the board sometimes can hinder rather than help. Black's own pawn at h3 obstructs his King, whereupon he gets mated: 1. Nf3 h2 2. Nf2. Erase Black's pawn from the board at the start, however, and there is no forced mate. In order to mate Black's King, White must first trap it on one move (stalemating), and then deliver a mating check on the next move. But without that extra pawn to give Black a free move, he is stalemated one move before he is mated, which is why two knights alone cannot mate.

1. Nf3   h2
2. Nf2   mate
(1–0)

ENDGAME **157**

W: Kg4, Nd2, Nf1 **B:** Kg1, Pf2
White moves and wins

Mate in Three Moves

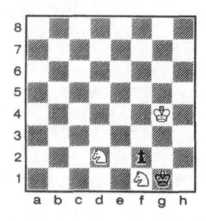

Black's pawn is firmly blocked by the Knight at f1, which in turn is guarded by the other horse at d2. White, in fact, could play to win the pawn, but what a mistake: 1. Kf3 Kh1 2. Kxf2 stalemate. It's much better to leave the pawn on the board, where it helps to imprison Black's King. The right idea is 1. **Kh3**, and after 1. . . .**Kh1**, White forces mate in two more moves with 2. **Ng3+ Kg1** 3. **Nf3**.

1.	**Kh3**	**Kh1**
2.	**Ng3 +**	**Kg1**
3.	**Nf3**	**mate**

(1–0)

ENDGAME **158**

W: Kg6, Nd7, Nh2 **B:** Kg8, Ph3
White moves and wins

Mate in Four Moves

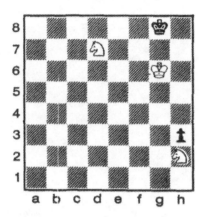

Black's King is ambushed in the upper right-hand corner of the board, pacing back and forth between h8 and g8. To finish him, White must enlist the blockading Knight at h2. Once the h2-Knight gallops in, however, it frees Black's pawn to head for promotion. White, of course, cannot win if he captures the pawn, for a stalemate arrives one move before delivering mate. But a simple calculation shows that White can afford to ignore the h-pawn's movement, letting it gain Queenship. This gives White just enough time to tighten the net, and mate Black one move after the Queening. An alterntive solution is 1. Ng4 h2 2. Ngf6+ Kh8 3. Ne5 h1/Q 4. Nf7 mate.

1.	Ng4	h2
2.	Nh6+	Kh8
3.	Nf6	h1/Q
4.	Nf7	mate

(1–0)

12

Minor Piece plus Pawn

ENDGAME 159

W: Kh5, Bh8, Pf3 B: Kf5
White moves and wins

Critical Square 1

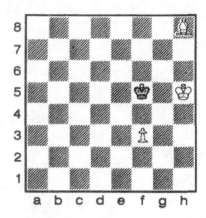

Black threatens to draw by 1. . . . Kf4, followed by capture of White's pawn, squashing White's hopes of making a new Queen. Without the pawn, White can't win, for a Bishop and King partnership cannot mate a lone enemy King; Black couldn't even blunder into mate. White therefore plans to keep the pawn, whatever the cost. Thus, the expendable Bishop is sacrificed, 1. Be5, preventing Black from attacking the pawn. White's King is empowered to position on the critical square g5. The pawn is then chaperoned home.

1. Be5	Kxe5	7. f6	Kh8
2. Kg5	Ke6	8. Kf7	Kh7
3. f4	Kf7	9. Ke7	Kg6
4. Kf5	Ke7	10. f7	Kf5
5. Kg6	Kf8	11. f8/Q +	
6. f5	Kg8		(1–0)

ENDGAME **160**

W: Ke4 B: Kc6, Bh2, Pg3
White moves and draws

Misplaced Bishop

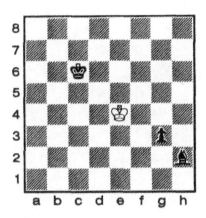

White is down a Bishop and pawn, dimming his position. Since he cannot permit the further advance of the g-pawn, his first few moves are forced: 1. **Kf3 Kd5** 2. **Kg2 Ke4** 3. **Kh1**. Amazingly, White's King is in just the right spot to prevent the blistering expression of Black's forces. Any attempt by Black to deny White access to g2 ends in stalemate. Nor can Black sacrifice his Bishop profitably, for 3. . . . .**Kf4** 4. **Kg2 Bg1** 5. **Kxg1** still ends in a draw.

1.	Kf3	Kd5
2.	Kg2	Ke4
3.	Kh1	Kf4
4.	Kg2	Bg1
5.	Kxg1	Kf3
6.	Kf1	g2 +
7.	Kg1	Kg3
	Stalemate	

ENDGAME 161

W: Kf1 B: Kg3, Be5, Ph3
White moves and draws

Wrong Color Bishop

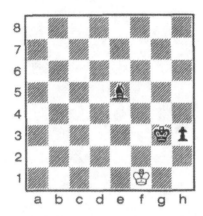

This is the age-old draw with the Rook-pawn and the wrong color Bishop. The matching Bishop on e5 operates only on dark squares, always unable to control the light-colored Queening square h1. After 1. **Kg1**, it makes no difference how Black plays. White's King is assured of reaching the Queening square, and since this is also a corner square, any attempt to squeeze him out produces a stalemate. If, in the diagram, Black's Bishop were on d5 instead of e5—that is, if it were a light-square Bishop—Black would win easily, for the Bishop could then guard White's niche at h1.

1. **Kg1** h2 +
2. **Kh1** Kf2
Stalemate

ENDGAME **162**

W: Kg6, Be7, Ph6 **B:** Kg8
White moves and wins

Right Color Bishop

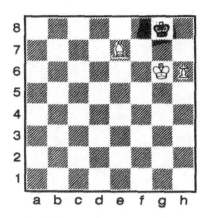

Even though White has a Rook-pawn, Black's cause is hopeless because White's Bishop controls the Queening square h8. Actually, checkmate is two moves away: 1. **h7+ Kh8** 2. **Bf6 mate.**

1. **h7+** **Kh8**
2. **Bf6** **mate**
(1–0)

ENDGAME **163**

W: Kc8, Bb4, Pa5 **B:** Ka6
White moves and wins

Critical Square 2

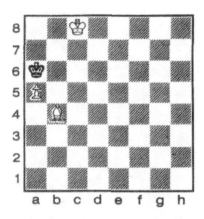

White's Bishop, traversing dark squares, performs the valuable function of bolstering the a-pawn. But given time, Black could play 1. . . .Ka7 and then 2. . . .Ka8, wedging into the corner. The Bishop then turns useless, since a8 is a light square, off limits to the Bishop, who can't guard it. White's King, though, is well placed, so it can first play to b8, halting Black's sprint for the corner. After 1. **Kb8 Kb5**   2. **Be1** (actually, White could play 2. Kb7 at once, abandoning his Bishop but Queening the pawn sooner) **Ka6**   3. **Bd2** (a tempo move, forcing Black to clear out) **Kb5**, White expels Black's King from a6 with 4. **Kb7**, occupying the a-pawn's critical square. The mere footman then strolls on.

1.	Kb8	Kb5
2.	Be1	Ka6
3.	Bd2	Kb5
4.	Kb7	

(1–0)

ENDGAME **164**

W: Kf3, Be4, Ph6 B: Kf7
White moves and wins

Critical-Square Fight

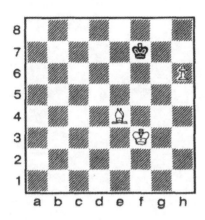

White's Bishop is the wrong color for his h-pawn. It doesn't control the Queening square, and Black's King has the possibility of finding haven at h8. But the King hasn't yet reached h8, though it threatens to play to g8 and then h8. With the paradoxical 1. **Bh7**, fronting to the h-pawn and temporarily blocking its advance, White is able to guard all approaches to the h8 corner. Black's last lunge is 1. . . .**Kf6**, trying to sneak behind the h-pawn by Kg5 next move. White's 2. **Kf4**, however, puts everything in order. White's King gradually moves up to dispirit Black's King away from h8. Eventually White's King hopes to occupy g7, the h-pawn's critical square, permitting the Bishop to move away and the h-pawn to proceed unmolested.

1.	**Bh7**	Kf6		6.	**Kf6**	Ke8
2.	**Kf4**	Ke6		7.	**Bg8**	Kf8
3.	**Kg5**	Kf7		8.	**h7**	Ke8
4.	**Kf5**	Ke7		9.	**h8/Q**	
5.	**Kg6**	Kf8			(1–0)	

ENDGAME **165**

Misplaced Bishop

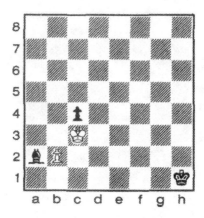

White's only drawing chance is to activate his b-pawn before Black cements it with 1. . . .Bb3. So White immediately plays 1. **b4**, threatening a missile to the Queening palace. Because Black's King is outside the "square of the pawn" at b4 (an imaginary box, here extending from b4 to b8 to f8 to f4), he can't possibly overtake the wing-footed b-pawn to catch it in time. And Black's Bishop can't be shanghaied to help either, for it is tied to protecting Black's only pawn. Black's only poor choice is to capture White's pawn. 1. . . .cxb3 en passant. But as we saw in Endgame 160, this position cannot be won, because as Black's King gets close to his Bishop and Pawn, he stalemates White.

1.	b4	cxb3	5. Kc1	Kd3
2.	Kb2	Kg2	6. Kb2	Kd2
3.	Kc1	Kf3	7. Ka1	Kc3
4.	Kb2	Ke2	Stalemate	

ENDGAME **166**

W: Kf6, Be5, Ph6 **B:** Kh8, Ph7
White moves and wins

Cornered

Black has mistakenly grabbed shelter in the h8 corner, where his own pawn at h7 helps to bring doom. White jousts in an instant mate, 1. **Kf7**. On the previous move, when Black's King was on g8, it should have gone to f8, not h8. That would have avoided the problem.

1. **Kf7** **mate**
(1–0)

ENDGAME 167

W: Kb1, Pa2 **B**: Kc3, Bd4, Pa3
White moves and draws

Avoid the Corner

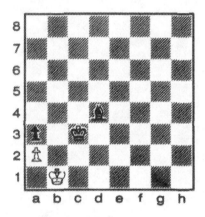

White stands his ground with 1. **Kc1** (not 1. Ka1, because of 1.
. . .Kc2 discovered mate). Any effort by Black to infiltrate causes
stalemate. For example: (a) 1. . . . .**Kd3**   2. **Kb1 Kd2**, or (B) 1.
. . .Be3+   2. Kb1 Kd2   3. Ka1 (here, this corner retreat is perfectly safe) Kc2.

1. **Kc1**   **Kd3**
2. **Kb1**   **Kd2**
Stalemate

ENDGAME **168**

W: Kf8, Pe6 B: Ka7, Be2, Pg6
White moves and draws

Square of the Pawn

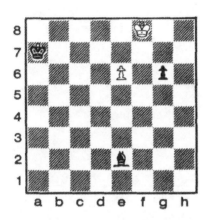

To achieve a draw, White must compound an attack on the g-pawn with a threat to Queen his e-pawn. What fuses the two ideas is the retreat along the critical diagonal a7–g1. White launches the unexpected 1. **Ke7**, blocking his e-pawn but with a threat to invade the "square of the g-pawn" (here, an imaginary box extending from g6 to g1 to b1 to b6). Black must advance his g-pawn: 1. . . .**g5** 2. **Kd6 g4** 3. **e7 Bb5**. Now 4. **Kc5** reveals the purpose of White's King march. Attacking the Bishop gains White a vital tempo to catch up with the g-pawn: 4. . . .**Bd7** 5. **Kd4**, and White's King has arrived within the desired box. The Black Bishop at d7 is overtaxed, guarding the g-pawn and fending off promotion of White's pawn at e8. The draw is salvaged by 5. . . .**Kb6** 6. **Ke4 Kc7** 7. **Kf4 Kd6** 8. **e8/Q Bxe8** 9. **Kxg4**, when Black's g-pawn keels over.

1.	Ke7	g5		6.	Ke4	Kc7
2.	Kd6	g4		7.	Kf4	Kd6
3.	e7	Bb5		8.	e8/Q	Bxe8
4.	Kc5	Bd7		9.	Kxg4	
5.	Kd4	Kb6			Draw	

ENDGAME **169**

W: Ke1 B: Kh1, Nd6, Ph2
White moves and draws

Color Rule

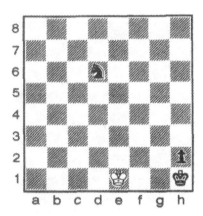

White must keep Black's King in the corner. If Black's King comes out he wins easily, Queening his h-pawn. White surely must play his King to the f-file, sealing Black in. Afterward, White's King can only shuttle back and forth between f2 and f1, where the Knight might try to drive it away. This the Knight does after 1. Kf1, for 1. . . .Ne4 immediately guards f2 and prevents White's King from moving there. But if White had started 1. **Kf2**, then whatever Black plays, he cannot prevent the perpetual pacing of White's King between f1 and f2. A color rule is helpful in such an instance. If you have the choice of moving to a Bishop-two square or a Bishop-one square to trap the King in the corner, move your King to the same color square as that occupied by the Knight. Since the Knight starts on d6, a dark square, White's King should go to f2, also a dark square. Had the Knight instead begun on e6, a light square, then White's King should have played to f1, a light square, too. That draws, regardless.

1.	Kf2	Ne4+	5. Kf2	Nd3+
2.	Kf1	Ng3+	6. Kf1	Ne1
3.	Kf2	Ne2	7. Kf2	Nf3
4.	Kf1	Nf4	8. Kf1	

Draw

ENDGAME **170**

W: Kc3 B: Kb7, Nb4, Pa3
White moves and draws

Force the Pawn to the 7th

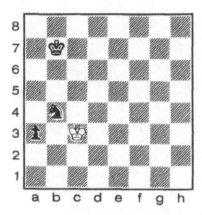

White must ignore the hanging Knight and not play 1. Kxb4?, when 1. . . .a2 Queens. He instead beams his attention on the a-pawn, 1. **Kb3**. This compels Black's advance of his pawn to the 7th rank, 1. . . .a2, after which the game cannot be won, for White's King can secrete itself in the corner at a1: 2. **Kb2 Kb6** 3. **Ka1**. The only way to pry White's King from the corner is to move the Knight to guard a1, but the Knight is committed to the defense of the a-pawn. And Black's King can come in just so far with help or else it's stalemate. Black can never safely guard the a-pawn to free the Knight and has no way to win.

1. **Kb3**   a2
2. **Kb2**   Kb6
3. **Ka1**   Kb5
4. **Kb2**   Ka4
5. **Ka1**   Ka3
   Stalemate

ENDGAME 171

W: Kh3, Ng4, Ph6 B: Kg6
White moves and wins

Avoiding Stalemate

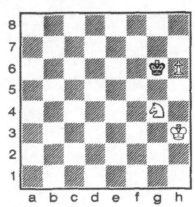

For the moment, White's Knight is chained to defensive duty, guarding the pawn on h6. By bringing his King up the board, 1. **Kh4 Kf7** 2. **Kg5** (or Kh5), White protects the pawn and releases the Knight for active relocation. The Knight must maneuver to f7 (not to f6, a blunder that often sets up stalemates) to guard h8. So the Knight jumps to e5 and then f7, after which White soon mates.

	A		**B**	
1.	Kh4	Kf7	Kh4	Kh7
2.	Kg5	Kg8	Kg5	Kh8
3.	Kg6	Kh8	Kg6	Kg8
4.	Ne5	Kg8	Ne5	Kh8
5.	h7 +	Kh8	Nf7 +	Kg8
6.	Nf7	mate	h7 +	Kf8
	(1–0)	7. h8/Q +	Ke7	
			8. Qd8 +	Ke6
			9. Qd6 +	mate
			(1–0)	

ENDGAME 172

Rear Defense

White's King is too far away to support his pawn, so the Knight assumes the task. It quickly gets back, 1. Ne6 Ka7 2. Nc5, defending the pawn from behind, so if the Knight were captured, the a-pawn could not be caught by Black's King. If instead White plays 2. Nc7, defending the pawn from in front, the protection dissipates after 2. . . .Kb6. If the Knight then stays where it is, Black can capture it and still get over in time to stop the pawn. Should the Knight flee, Black easily swallows the a-pawn. After defending the pawn from behind with the Knight, White's King moves up to protect the pawn additionally, freeing the Knight to guard a8. Black is powerless to fend off eventual mate.

1. Ne6	Ka7	6. Kb5	Ka8	11. a8/Q+	Kd7
2. Nc5	Kb6	7. Kb6	Kb8	12. Qe8+	Kd6
3. Kb3	Ka7	8. Ne6	Ka8	13. Qe6	mate
4. Kb4	Kb6	9. Nc7+	Kb8	(1–0)	
5. Kc4	Ka7	10. a7+	Kc8		

ENDGAME 173

W: Ke1, Ph2 **B:** Kf3, Ne4, Ph3
White moves and draws

Corner Curl up

Thanks to the Rook-pawns, White builds a fortress in the h1 corner that defies penetration. For example, 1. **Kf1** Nf2 2. **Kg1** Ke2 is stalemate. Black's best try is to set up a trap that might lure a careless opponent: 1. . . .**Ng3+**, hoping for 2. hxg3, when 2. . . .h2 makes a new Queen by force. But White might be too shrewd to bite the Knight, and he can simply head for the corner with his King. The Rook-pawns are the real problem and prevent Black from winning. If all the pieces and pawns were shifted one file toward the Queenside, it would be a different picture. Then it becomes an easy win, as we shall see in Endgame 175.

1. **Kf1**   **Ng3+**
2. **Kg1**   **Ne2+**
3. **Kh1**
         Draw

ENDGAME **174**

W: Ke6, Ne7, Ph6 **B:** Ke8, Ph7
White moves and wins

King and Knight Duel

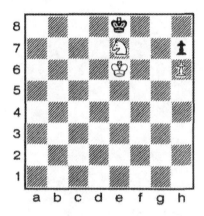

Black's King has not yet departed into his citadel at h8, nor is it clear how it can, with White's Knight lording over g8 from e7. But White still needs some way to breach Black's position: 1. Kd6 Kf7 2. Kd7 Kf8 3. Ke6 Ke8 4. Kf6 Kf8, and White has not been able to dent Black's front lines. The sacrificial 1. **Ng6!** is the oracle's answer. Progress is swift after 1. . . .Kd8 2. Kf7, for White's King penetrates. And after 1. . . .**hxg6**, the h-pawn trumpets forward to make a new Queen.

1 Ng6   hxg6
2. h7   Kf8
3. h8/Q   mate
(1–0)

ENDGAME 175

W: Ke6, Nh5, Pg6 B: Kh8, Pg7
White moves and wins

Curled up

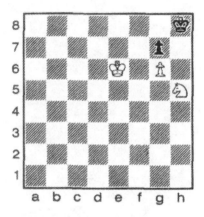

With Black's King in the corner, White must be wary of stalemate traps, such as 1. Kf7?, leaving Black with no move. The
winning idea is to smother Black's King with the Knight, 1. **Nf6!**,
so that the pawn must capture the Knight, 1. . . .**gxf6**. The
capture frees White's g-pawn to menace. After 2. **Kf7**, Black is
trapped and can move only his f-pawn. White soon mates.

1. Nf6	gxf6
2. Kf7	f5
3. g7 +	Kh7
4. g8/Q +	Kh6
5. Qg6	mate

(1–0)

ENDGAME **176**

W: Kc5, Na8, Pb5 **B:** Kb7, Pc7
White moves and wins

Outflanking

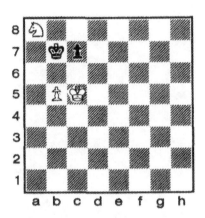

White's Knight is on one of its four worst squares. It can move to just two places from any corner. Here the poor hoofer faces capture for nothing. A sacrifice for a pawn, 1. Nxc7, fails to 1. ...Kxc7, and White gets nowhere. Oddly, the Knight really should be yielded but not for immediate material gain. Rather, 1. Nb6! sets up a winning outflanking after 1. ...cxb6+ 2. Kd6. Black's b-pawn then keels over by force, and White hails a new Queen.

1.	Nb6	cxb6 +
2.	Kd6	Kb8
3.	Kc6	Ka7
4.	Kc7	Ka8
5.	Kxb6	Kb8
6.	Ka6	Ka8
7.	b6	Kb8
8.	b7	Kc7
9.	Ka7	Kc6
10.	b8/Q	

(1–0)

13

Heavy Pieces

ENDGAME 177

W: Kd1, Re7, Pc2 B: Kc3, Qf4
White moves and wins

The Fortress

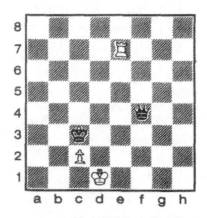

Black insinuates mate at d2. If White's Rook guards d2 from d7, then the Queen mates at f1. The defense 1. Re2 also loses after 1. . . .Qd4+, when both (A) 2. Kc1 Qg1+ 3. Re1 Qxe1, and (B) 2. Ke1 Qg1 are mate. White melds the position as 1. **Re3+!**. Capturing the Rook with the Queen, 1. . . . Qxe3, is stalemate. And if Black's King ventures forward, 1. . . .**Kb2**, the Rook keeps away disaster with 2. **Rb3+ Ka2** 3. **Rd3**, when White's c-pawn anchors the castle securely at b3 or d3. Queen checks add up to nothing, and Black's King is rebuked from participating by checks and cut-offs. Black cannot force a win.

1.	Re3+	Kb2
2.	Rb3+	Ka2
3.	Rd3	

Draw

W: Ke5, Qf1, Pd5 B: Kd8, Rd6, Pc7
White moves and wins

Breaking Down the Fortress 1

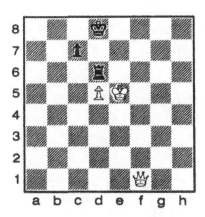

White's Queen is worth more than Black's Rook, but with the Rook protected by the c-pawn, White's King cannot make an entrance, and his assistance is normally required to threaten Black seriously. Perhaps some alchemy would pay off. White should give up the golden Queen for the baser Rook. After 1. **Qf8 + Kd7** 2. **Qxd6 + ! cxd6 +** 3. **Kf6**, Black is outflanked and loses his pawn. White's pawn is then elevated to a Queen.

1.	Qf8 +	Kd7
2.	Qxd6 +	cxd6 +
3.	Kf6	Kd8
4.	Ke6	Kc7
5.	Ke7	Kc8
6.	Kxd6	Kd8
7.	Ke6	Ke8
8.	d6	Kd8
9.	d7	Kc7
10.	Ke7	Kc6
11.	d8/Q	

(1–0)

ENDGAME 179

W: Kh5, Qb4, Pg5 B: Ke8, Rg6, Pf7
White moves and wins

Breaking Down the Fortress 2

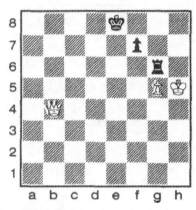

Once again, the Black Rook cuts off White's King, but White's Queen rescues with 1. **Qe4+**, confronting Black with two losing responses. He can block the check on the e-file, 1. . . . **Re6**, but after 2. **Qxe6+ fxe6** 3. **Kh6**, White Queens a pawn at least two moves ahead of Black. Or Black could escape toward the Kingside, 1. . . . **Kf8**, when 2. **Qxg6+ fxg6+** 3. **Kxg6** establishes White's king on a critical square for the g5-pawn, ensuring victory whatever Black decides to play.

	A	
1.	Qe4+	Kf8
2.	Qxg6+	fxg6+
3.	Kxg6	Kg8
4.	Kh6	Kh8
5.	g6	Kg8
6.	g7	Kf7
7.	Kh7	Kf6
8.	g8/Q	
	(1–0)	

	B	
1.	Qe4+	Re6
2.	Qxe6+	fxe6
3.	Kh6	e5
4.	g6	e4
5.	g7	Kf7
6.	Kh7	e3
7.	g8/Q+	
	(1–0)	

W: Kf1, Qh3, Pf7 B: Ka2, Qf8
White moves and wins

Lifting the Blockade 1

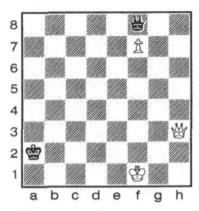

If given time free from opposing checks, White wins in similar situations by goaling his Queen to the 8th rank under protection of its pawn and breaking the Black Queen's blockade. But how does White's Queen get to the 8th rank without losing time or the pawn, now threatened by the Black Queen? The win hinges on check. After 1. **Qe6 +**, protecting the pawn and preparing transfer to e8, Black is done in. If 1. . . .**Kb2**, then 2. **Qe8 Qb4** 3. **f8/Q Qc4 +** 4. **Qe2 + Qxe2 +** 5. **Kxe2** leaves White with the only Queen. An alternative win, though slightly longer, begins with 1. **Qg2 +** followed by 2. **Qg8.** That operation also lifts the blockade.

1.	Qe6 +	Kb2
2.	Qe8	Qb4
3.	f8/Q	Qc4 +
4.	Qe2 +	Qxe2 +
5.	Kxe2	

(1–0)

ENDGAME **181**

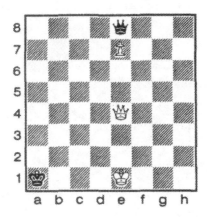

W: Ke1, Qe4, Pe7 **B:** Ka1, Qe8
White moves and wins

Lifting the Blockade 2

Blockade-breaking starts with a check. After 1. **Qd4+ Kb1,**
Black's Queen is forced out by 2. **Qe8.** The Black Queen must
subside—it doesn't have a check—and White makes a new
Queen. If Black's Queen begins checking, White will soon
trade Queens with a cross-check (blocking a check and giving a
check with the same piece on the same move). Should Black
somehow avoid the Queen trade, White would trap and mate
Black's King anyway.

> 1. **Qd4+**   **Kb1**
> 2. **Qd8**
>
> (1–0)

ENDGAME **182**

W: Ke7, Qg6, Pf7 B: Kc8, Qe3
White moves and wins

Cross-Check 1

A key resource to stop enemy Queen checks is to give a cross-check—block a check with a check. After 1. **Qe6 + Qxe6 +** 2. **Kxe6,** Black is helpless to halt the f-pawn's advance to become a new Queen.

1. **Qe6 +**   **Qxe6 +**
2. **Kxe6**   **Kc7**
3. **f8/Q**
(1–0)

ENDGAME **183**

W: Kg7, Qg6, Pe7 **B:** Ka1, Qd7
White moves and wins

Cross-Check 2

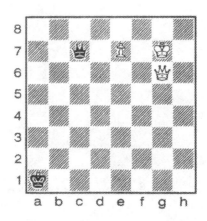

Black is staking his defense on pinning White's e-pawn, which is immobilized and threatened by Black's Queen. When White breaks the pin, 1. **Qf7**, Black must check, 1. . . . **Qg3+** (1. . . . Qc3+ is answered by the winning pin 2. Qf6); but after 2. **Kf8**, Black must resort to a diagonal pin, 2. . . . **Qa3**. White eases out of the pin, 3. **Kg8**, and seeks to make a new Queen. If Black continues with 3. . . . **Qg4+**, the only real nuisance move, White responds with a simplifying cross-check, 4. **Qg7+**, forcing a trade of Queens and putting an end to Black's drawing attempts.

1.	Qf7	Qg3 +
2.	Kf8	Qa3
3.	Kg8	Qg3 +
4.	Qg7 +	Qxg7 +
5.	Kxg7	

(1–0)

ENDGAME **184**

W: Kg8, Qa4 **B:** Kb1, Qe5, Pb2
White moves and draws

Perpetual Check

The defending Queen's almost magical weapon is perpetual check—the ability to check the opposing King endlessly. Though mate cannot be forced in this manner, perpetual check prevents the superior side from proceeding with his plans. His every move must get him out of check instead of delivering mate or making a new Queen. The best way to ward off perpetual check generally is to place your own Queen on a central square, for that reduces the opposing Queen's attacking possibilities. Here, Black's Queen is in the center, but it still can't stop the incessant checking of White's Queen from a4 to d1 and back, over and over. The game is drawn by the threefold repetition rule, which permits a player to claim a draw if he is about to repeat the same position for the third time.

1. Qd1+ Ka2
2. Qa4+ Kb1
3. Qd1+ Ka2
4. Qa4+ Kb1
   Draw

14

Heavy Pieces: Rooks

ENDGAME **185**

W: Kb3, Ra8, Pa7 B: Kf7, Ra1
White moves and wins

Skewer 1

You will find this position offers only seven safe squares for Black's King. Five are near the a7-pawn—b7, c7, a6, b6, and c6; the other two are g7 and h7. Other squares would only place Black's King in check to White's advantage, or where it could be exploited tactically. Since the Black King is not on a safe square, he pays through the nose: 1. **Rh8 Rxa7** (otherwise the pawn Queens) 2. **Rh7+ Kg6** 3. **Rxa7**. White's skewer to Black's King and Rook wins a Rook. If in the initial position it were Black's move, he would play King to g7, avoiding the skewer and drawing. White's Rook on a8 would simply have no outlet. If White brought up his King to release the Rook from defense of the a-pawn, Black's Rook would commence checking. Where, then, would White's King go to hide from checks—the moon?

	1.	Rh8	Rxa7
	2.	Rh7+	Kg6
	3.	Rxa7	

(1–0)

ENDGAME **186**

W: Ka4, Rh8 **B:** Kb2, Rh1, Ph2
White moves and wins

Hiding

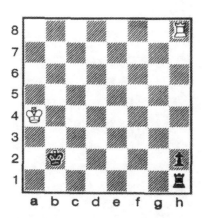

White's King must seek shelter from the gunfire threat of 1. . . .Ra1+, followed by 2. . . .h1/Q. The only place to hide is on the b-file, in the shadow of Black's King: 1. **Kb4!**. Since Black's Rook has to protect his pawn, Black's only chance is to march his King across the board to support the pawn, releasing the Rook. White's King has to match it: 1. . . .**Kc2** 2. **Kc4 Kd2** 3. **Kd4 Ke2** 4. **Ke4 Kf2** 5. **Kf4 Kg2**. Once Black's Rook is free to move without risking pawn loss, White must check, 6. **Rg8+ Kh3** 7. **Rh8+ Kg2** 8. **Rg8+**, and Black's a goner. Still, he tries 8. . . .**Kf2** 9. **Rh8 Rf1**, but this fails to 10. **Rxh2+ Kg1+** 11. **Kg3**, when White's King returns to defend his Rook. Note how this caper would have been a successful one if on White's first move he had essayed 1. Kb5?, assuming that to draw it would be sufficient to shelter his King anywhere on the b-file. After 1. Kb5?, Black *triumphs* with 1. . . .Kc3! 2. Kc5 Kd3 3. Kd5 Ke3 4. Ke5 Kf3 5. Kf5 Rf1 6. Rxh2 Kg3+, for White's Rook is lost.

1.	**Kb4**	**Kc2**	5.	**Kf4**	**Kg2**	9.	**Rh8**	**Rf1**
2.	**Kc4**	**Kd2**	6.	**Rg8+**	**Kh3**	10.	**Rxh2+**	**Kg1+**
3.	**Kd4**	**Ke2**	7.	**Rh8+**	**Kg2**	11.	**Kg3**	
4.	**Ke4**	**Kf2**	8.	**Rg8+**	**Kf2**		Draw	

ENDGAME 187

W: Kc4, Ra8, Pa7 B: Ke5, Re7
White moves and wins

Zugzwang

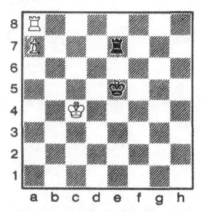

Black's Rook performs double duty—guarding his King from checks on the e-file and keeping the a-pawn under attack, preventing White's pawn from moving away. With 1. **Kc5!** White strains Black's defense to the limit, *zugzwang*ing him so that however he moves, his position deteriorates. For example: (A) 1. . . .**Rc7+** 2. **Kb6** enables White to move his Rook away, clearing the promotion square; or (B) 1. . . . **Ke6** 2. **Kb6** causes Black's King to block his Rook from checking along the rank; of (C) 1. . . . **Ke4** 2. **Kd6**, which, if Black's Rook departs the e-file, gains White's Rook time to free the pawn by checking at e8. However Black continues, he must self-destruct, which is the charm of *zugzwang* positions.

A		B		C	
1. Kc5	Rc7+	1. Kc5	Ke6	1. Kc5	Ke4
2. Kb6		2. Kb6		2. Kd6	
(1–0)		(1–0)		(1–0)	

ENDGAME **188**

W: Kc3, Rg8 **B:** Kh1, Re7, Ph2
White moves and draws

Shut In

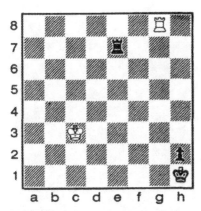

White's Rook at g8 blocks the g-file, imprisoning Black's King at h1. Black wants to shoo White's Rook by 1. . . .Re1, followed by 2. . . .Rg1. White's first move is therefore forced: 1. **Kd2**, guarding e1. Black, meanwhile, approaches the same problem differently. His Rook can shift to the a-file, then the 1st rank, then to g1. But after 1. . . .**Ra7**, White's King can speed back, 2. **Ke2 Ra1** 3. **Kf2**, so that 3. . . .**Rg1** is ineffectual. Though White's Rook must yield the g-file, his King is close enough to shut in Black's King. Simplest now is 4. **Rf8**, to prevent checking of White's King off the f-file. Black can check at g2, 4. . . .**Rg2+**, but this check dissolves after 5. **Kf1**. White's King cannot be dislodged from both f2 and f1, so Black's sovereign can never exit the corner.

1.	**Kd2**	**Ra7**
2.	**Ke2**	**Ra1**
3.	**Kf2**	**Rg1**
4.	**Rf8**	**Rg2+**
5.	**Kf1**	

Draw

ENDGAME 189

W: Ka8, Rh8, Pa7 B: Kd7, Rb1
White moves and wins

Driving Off

Black's King hasn't reached c7, so White has time to extricate his King from the corner. First he takes the b-file, 1. **Rb8**, forcing Black's Rook off, 1. . . .**Rc1**. Then White's monarch comes out, 2. **Kb7**, ready to aid his pawn to Queen. Black's Rook whips out serial checks, 2. . . .**Rb1+**, but these are useless after 3. **Ka6 Ra1+** 4. **Kb6 Rb1+** 5. **Kc5 Rc1+** 6. **Kd4 Rd1+** 7. **Ke3 Re1+** 8. **Kd2**. The checks ended, the a-pawn certainly Queens.

1.	Rb8	Rc1
2.	Kb7	Rb1+
3.	Ka6	Ra1+
4.	Kb6	Rb1+
5.	Kc5	Rc1+
6.	Kd4	Rd1+
7.	Ke3	Re1+
8.	Kd2	

Draw

ENDGAME **190**

Back-Rank Escape

W: Ka8, Rh8, Pa7 B: Kd6, Rb1
White moves and wins

White challenges the b-file in an effort to excavate his King from the corner, 1. **Rb8 Rc1** 2. **Kb7**. But now Black's King at d6 hinders the White King from escaping checks over the files, as in 2. . . .**Rb1+** 3. **Ka6 Ra1+** 4. **Kb6 Rb1+**, and so on. The White King, therefore, rushes to the back rank, 2. . . .**Rb1+** 3. **Kc8 Rc1+** 4. **Kd8**. After 4. . . .**Rh1**, however, Black glowers mate at h8. For White to answer 5. **Ke8** would be futile, because of the skewer 5. . . .**Rh8+** 6. **Kf7 Rh7+**, followed by 7. . . .**Rxa7**. But White can offer 5. **Rb6+**, when 5. . . .**Kc5** is countered by 6. **Rc6+**. Now if Black swallows the Rook, White Queens with check. So Black is stuck with 6. . . .**Kb5**, when 7. **Rc8 Rh8+** 8. **Kc7 Rh7+** 9. **Kb8** leaves him no adequate way to oppose the marching pawn.

1. **Rb8**	**Rc1**	6. **Rc6+**	**Kb5**
2. **Kb7**	**Rb1+**	7. **Rc8**	**Rh8+**
3. **Kc8**	**Rc1+**	8. **Kc7**	**Rh7+**
4. **Kd8**	**Rh1**	9. **Kb8**	
5. **Rb6+**	**Kc5**	(1–0)	

ENDGAME **191**

W: Kc8, Rd2, Pc7 B: Ke7, Rc1
White moves and wins

Escaping Along the File

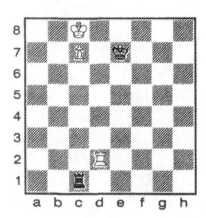

White's pawn is one little square away from Queendom, but his King needs to step clear safely. The rightside exit is blocked by Black's King, but a leftside side step might work. A Queenside walk for White, however, might run him into barraging checks after 1. Kb7 Rb1 + 2. Kc6 Rc1 + 3. Kb6 Rb1 + 4. Ka5 Ra1 +, and so on, forcing the King back to c8. It's totally sensible for White's Rook to usurp the b-file, 1. **Rb2.** Black has nothing better than a temporizing 1. . . .Rc3, and then White implements his winning plan: 2. **Kb7 Kd7** 3. **c8/Q + Rxc8** 4. **Rd2 + Ke6** 5. **Kxc8,** emerging with an extra Rook.

1.	Rb2	Rc3
2.	Kb7	Kd7
3.	c8/Q +	Rxc8
4.	Rd2 +	Ke6
5.	Kxc8	

(1–0)

ENDGAME **192**

W: Kc8, Rd2, Pc7 **B:** Ke7, Rb1
White moves and wins

Breaking the Cut-off

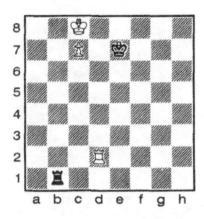

Black's Rook holds the b-file, preventing escape of White's King to the Queenside. White can drive off Black's Rook, however, using the a-file as a conduit: 1. **Ra2 Rb3** (waiting for White to do something) 2. **Ra7 Rb1** 3. **Rb7**. Black's Rook can do no less than give way; White's King moves off the promotion square, and Black has to sacrifice his Rook for White's pawn, 3. . . .**Rc1** 4. **Kb8 Kd7** 5. **c8/Q+**, and the double-check proves decisive. Another winning idea from the initial position is: 1. **Ra2 Rb3** 2. **Ra8 Rb1** 3. **Rb8 Rc1** 4. **Kb7 Rb1+** 5. **Ka6 Ra1+** 6. **Kb5 Rb1+** 7. **Ka4 Ra1+** 8. **Kb3 Rb1+** 9. **Kc2**, and Black's checking days are over.

1.	**Ra2**	**Rb3**
2.	**Ra7**	**Rb1**
3.	**Rb7**	**Rc1**
4.	**Kb8**	**Kd7**
5.	**c8/Q+**	

(1–0)

ENDGAME **193**

W: Kb8, Rc1, Pb7 **B:** Kd7, Ra2
White moves and wins

The Bridge

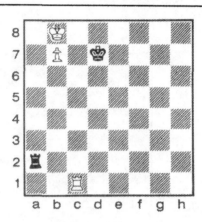

With a Knight-pawn on the 7th rank, White lacks a maneuverable challenge to Black's Rook on the Rook-file. So he goes to work against the Black King, 1. **Rd2+**. Black backs off, 1. . . .**Ke7**, since alternatives are worse: (A) 1. . . .Kc6 2. Kc8, and the pawn Queens; or (B) 1. . . .Ke6 2. Kc8 Rc1+ 3. Kd8 Rb1 4. Rd7, and White threatens 5. Kc8, 6. Rc7, and 7. b8/Q. White continues in the main line (listed below) with 2. **Rd4**, beginning the process called "building a bridge." After Black tempos with 2. . . .**Ra2**, White's King emerges 3. **Kc7 Rc2+** 4. **Kb6 Rb2+** 5. **Ka6** (also good is 5. Kc6). Further Black Rook checks are useless, for 5. . . .Ra2+ is met by 6. Kb5 Rb2+ 7. Rb4, revealing that White's second move was played to create a block against Rook checks on the b-file. After 5. **Ka6**, White means to transfer his Rook to the 5th rank, then over to the b-file to protect his King from checks. Black closes in with his King, 5. . . .**Ke6**, but White still wins with 6. **Ra4**, safeguarding his King from checks along the a-file. Black loses his Rook for the pawn after 6. . . .**Kd6** 7. **Ka7 Kc7** 8. **b8/Q+ Rxb8** 9. **Rc4+ Kd6** 10. **Kxb8**.

1.	**Rd2+**	**Ke7**	5.	**Ka6**	**Ke6**	9.	**Rc4+**	**Kd6**
2.	**Rd4**	**Ra2**	6.	**Ra4**	**Kd6**	10.	**Kxb8**	
3.	**Kc7**	**Rc2+**	7.	**Ka7**	**Kc7**		(1–0)	
4.	**Kb6**	**Rb2+**	8.	**b8/Q+**	**Rxb8**			

ENDGAME **194**

W: Ke8, Rf1, Pe7 **B:** Kg7, Rb8
White moves and wins

Preventing the Checking Distance

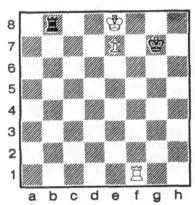

Black tries to draw by attacking White's King from the flank. This valid defense might succeed if Black's Rook were one file farther left of White's pawn. As it is, the Rook is too close and White gains a vital tempo, turning the game in his favor: 1. **Kd7 Rb7+** 2. **Kd8 Rb8+** 3. **Kc7 Ra8**. When a Rook is far enough from the pawn it is attacking (at least three files must lie between Rook and pawn to be effective), it has "checking distance." Black's Rook has just gotten the checking distance at a8, when three files—the b-, c-, and d-files—divide it from the pawn. But it is White's move, and he can prevent Black from capitalizing on it with 4. **Ra1!**. If Black takes the Rook, White will Queen, so he instead loses by 4. . . .**Re8** 5. **Kd7 Kf7** 6. **Rf1+ Kg7** 7. **Kxe8.**

1.	**Kd7**	**Rb7+**
2.	**Kd8**	**Rb8+**
3.	**Kc7**	**Ra8**
4.	**Ra1**	**Re8**
5.	**Kd7**	**Kf7**
6.	**Rf1+**	**Kg7**
7.	**Kxe8**	

(1–0)

W: Kg2, Ra7 B: Ke1, Rf8, Pe2
White moves and wins

Flank Attack 1

White's flank attack succeeds here because the three empty files between the Rook and Black's pawn give White's Rook the vital checking distance: 1. **Ra1 +** **Kd2** 2. **Ra2 +** **Kd3** 3. **Ra3 + Kd4**, enabling Rook to torment Black's King. White now must check from a4, since pulling his Rook back to the first rank, 4. Ra1, loses to 4. . . .Ra8! 5. Rb1 Kd3 6. Kf2 Rf8+ 7. Kg2 Kd2 8. Rb2+ Kd1 9. Rb1+ Kc2 10. Ra1 Ra8!, and Black wins, as did White in the previous endgame. But 4. **Ra4 +** holds for 4. . . .Kd5 5. Ra1 Ra8 6. Re1 Re8 7. Kf2 picks off the e-pawn. A draw also ensues after 4. . . .Kc3 5. **Ra3 +** **Kb2** 6. **Re3**, again snaring the pawn.

1.	**Ra1 +**	**Kd2**
2.	**Ra2 +**	**Kd3**
3.	**Ra3 +**	**Kd4**
4.	**Ra4 +**	**Kc3**
5.	**Ra3 +**	**Kb2**
6.	**Re3**	
	Draw	

ENDGAME **196**

W: Ke8, Rf1, Pe7 B: Kg8, Ra8
White moves and wins

Bad King's Position

Black's Rook has the proper checking distance to sustain a successful flank attack, but his King's position on g8 is a spoiler. White wins with either of two methods. One is to play his King to the Queenside: 1. **Kd7 Ra7+** 2. **Kd6 Ra6+** 3. **Kc5** (this is possible because 3. . . . Re6 runs into 4. Rf8+) **Ra8** 4. **Kc6 Kg7** (too late) 5. **Ra1!** (preventing Black from utilizing checking distance to attack the flank) **Rb8** 6. **Kc7 Re8** 7. **Kd7 Kf7** 8. **Rf1+ Kg7** 9. **Kxe8**, winning a Rook. In the other approach, White's King circles around to the Kingside: 1. **Kd7 Ra7+** 2. **Ke6 Ra6+** 3. **Ke5 Ra5+** 4. **Kf6 Ra6+** 5. **Kg5 Ra5+** 6. **Kg6 Ra6+** 7. **Rf6! Ra8** 8. **Rd6 Re8** 9. **Rd8 Rxd8** 10. **exd8/Q mate.**

	A			**B**	
1.	Kd7	Ra7+	1.	Kd7	Ra7+
2.	Kd6	Ra6+	2.	Ke6	Ra6+
3.	Kc5	Ra8	3.	Ke5	Ra5+
4.	Kc6	Kg7	4.	Kf6	Ra6+
5.	Ra1	Rb8	5.	Kg5	Ra5+
6.	Kc7	Re8	6.	Kg6	Ra6+
7.	Kd7	Kf7	7.	Rf6	Ra8
8.	Rf1+	Kg7	8.	Rd6	Re8
9.	Kxe8		9.	Rd8	Rxd8 (1–0)
			10.	exd8/Q mate	
				(1–0)	

ENDGAME **197**

W: Kg1, Rb4 B: Kh3, Ra2, Pg3
White moves and draws

Passive Defense Draws 1

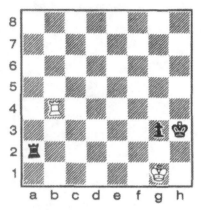

A mate threatens White (1. . . . Ra1), forcing his Rook to a passive position, 1. **Rb1**, defending his 1st rank. But as Black has a Knight-pawn and no maneuverability on the right of the pawn, the passive stance of White's Rook sufficiently holds the game. Black cannot effectively threaten, so White merely rickracks his Rook along the 1st rank. Black's best is 1. . . . **Rg2+**, hoping for White to blunder with 2. Kf1?. Then Black really has something after 2. . . . Kh2, preparing 3. . . . Rf2+, 4. . . . Rf8, and 5. . . . g2. But after 1. . . . **Rg2+**, White's King goes to the corner, 2. **Kh1**, and Black gets nowhere with 2. . . . **Rh2+** 3. **Kg1 Ra2** 4. **Rc1**. Note that if Black answers 3. **Kg1** with 3. . . . g2?, White snaps his Rook by 4. Rb3+.

1.	**Rb1**	**Rg2+**
2.	**Kh1**	**Rh2+**
3.	**Kg1**	**Ra2**
4.	**Rc1**	

Draw

ENDGAME 198

W: Kb6, Rb7, Pc6 B: Ka8, Rg8
White moves and wins

Passive Defense Loses 1

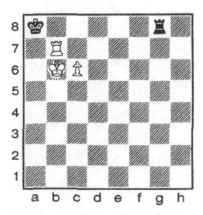

Black's Rook defends passively on the first rank. "Passive defense" means that the Rook's sole function is to prevent a mating check along the back rank. Counterattack is out of the question. Passive defense works if the advancing enemy footman is a Rook-pawn or a Knight-pawn. But passive defense fails against a Bishop-pawn or a center-pawn. White's Rook can sufficiently maneuver in the latter two cases to operate on the narrow side of the pawn (where fewer files separate the pawn from the edge) to win. After 1. **Ra7+ Kb8** 2. **c7+ Kc8**, White's Rook drops to the back row and skewers the enemy King and Rook, winning the Rook behind the King: 3. **Ra8+ Kd7** 4. **Rxg8** completely stomps Black.

1. **Ra7+**   **Kb8**
2. **c7+**   **Kc8**
3. **Ra8+**   **Kd7**
4. **Rxg8**
(1–0)

ENDGAME **199**

W: Ke1, Rc2 B: Ke3, Rh3, Pd3
White moves and draws

Stalemate Trick

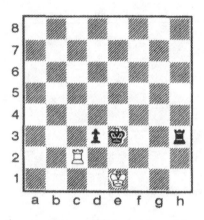

Black has two threats (1. . . . Rh1 mate and 1 . . . . dxc2). Both can be met by 1. **Re2+**, since 1 . . . . dxe2 is stalemate. If Black's King withdraws, 1. . . . **Kd4**, then 2. **Re8** prepares a round of checks from the rear: 2. . . . **Rh1+** 3. **Kd2 Rh2+** 4. **Kd1 Kc3** 5. **Rc8+ Kd4** 6. **Rd8+ Ke4** 7. **Re8+ Kf4** 8. **Rd8**, and Black must hang on a draw. When the defending King (here, White) stands in front of an enemy pawn advanced to its 6th rank, the attacking King (here, Black) won't find shelter from Rook checks from the rear, because there is no room in front of the pawn. Nor does it help to build a protective bridge, bringing the Black Rook back to block checks, for after the exchange of Rooks the King and pawn endgame is also drawn.

1.	Re2+	Kd4
2.	Re8	Rh1+
3.	Kd2	Rh2+
4.	Kd1	Kc3
5.	Rc8+	Kd4
6.	Rd8+	Ke4
7.	Re8+	Kf4
8.	Rd8	

Draw

ENDGAME **200**

W: Kg4, Rf1, Pg6 B: Ke7, Rf8
White moves and wins

Maintaining the Barrier

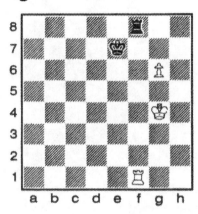

Black's King is cut off from the Queening file, and thereby unable to occupy a square in the enemy pawn's path. But if his Rook contests the f-file, White's Rook might move away or Rooks be exchanged, allowing King passage to the g-file. For example, both (A) 1. Re1+ Kf6   2. Rf1+ Kg7, as well as (B) 1. Rxf8 Kxf8   2. Kg5 Kg7 are drawn endgames. White forges a win, however, by maintaining his f-file grip: 1. **Rf5!**, so that 1. . . . Rxf5   2. Kxf5 Ke8   3. Ke6 Kf8   4. Kf6 Kg8 leads to the victorious squeeze of 5. g7 Kh7   6. Kf7. Black fares no better by answering 1. Rf5 with 1. . . . Rf6, for 2. **Kg5** forces Black to react unfavorably. After 2. . . . Ra6, White wins with 3. **g7 Ra1**   4. **Kg6** (not 4. g8/Q? because of 4. . . . Rg1+, pilfering the new Queen) **Rg1+**   5. **Kh7 Rh1+**   6. **Kg8 Rh2**   7. **Rf4**, which brings White to a position in which he can build a bridge, as in Endgame 193.

1. **Rf5**	**Rf6**		5. **Kh7**	**Rh1 +**
2. **Kg5**	**Ra6**		6. **Kg8**	**Rh2**
3. **g7**	**Ra1**		7. **Rf4**	
4. **Kg6**	**Rg1 +**			(1–0)

ENDGAME **201**

	W: Kg2, Re8 **B:** Ke2, Re1, Pe3
	White moves and draws

Flank Attack 2

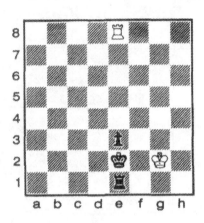

Given just one move (1. . . . Ra1), Black will untangle his piece lineup on the e-file. White must strike quickly with the best flank attack, 1. **Ra8!**, moving the Rook to the file farthest from the pawn to maintain its checking distance. Black gears to block checks by 1. . . . **Rd1**, after which may follow 2. **Ra2+ Rd2**, for 2. . . . Ke1 culls the stabilizing 3. Kf3. Now White's simplest defense is 3. **Ra1**, to keep Black's King off the 1st rank. Waiting moves, such as 3. . . . Rb2, 3. . . . Rc2, or 3. . . . Rd3, can be answered by a waiting move for White, 4. Kg3. There's no problem with 3. . . . Kd3+, for White gets a grip on the Queening square by 4. Kf1. Black tries 3. . . . **Rd1** 4. **Ra2+ Kd3** 5. **Ra3+ Ke4** 6. **Ra4+ Rd4**. An exchange of Rooks, 7. Rxd4+ Kxd4, would yield winning King and pawn endgame for Black after 8. Kf1 Kd3 9. Ke1 e2. But White evades the exchange with 7. **Ra8** (7. Ra1 is also good), and whether Black plays 7. . . . Rd2+ or 7. . . . Kd3, White draws easily with 8. **Kf1**, taking control of the Queening square.

1. **Ra8**	**Rd1**	4. **Ra2+**	**Kd3**	7. **Ra8**	**Kd3**
2. **Ra2+**	**Rd2**	5. **Ra3+**	**Ke4**	8. **Kf1**	
3. **Ra1**	**Rd1**	6. **Ra4+**	**Rd4**	Draw	

ENDGAME **202**

W: Kd7, Rd8, Pd6 **B:** Kf7, Ra1
White moves and wins

The Short-Side Problem

A basic for a successful flank attack is that three empty files (or ranks, as the case may be) separate the checking Rook from the adverse pawn. Thus the Rook can maintain its checking distance when attacking the rival King. The Rook and King must work as a team. The King should stand on the short side of the pawn to give the Rook maximum room on the long side of the pawn for checking distance. In this position, that teamwork is blatantly lacking and the Rook, checking on the short side, quickly comes to grief: 1. **Rc8 Ra7+** 2. **Kc6 Ra6+** (if 2. . . .Ke6, then 3. Re8+ and 4. d7) 3. **Kc7 Ra7+** 4. **Kb6**, and the checks run out. White wraps it up after 4. . . .Rd7 5. **Kc6 Ra7** 6. **Rc7+ Rxc7** 7. **dxc7**, making a new Queen next move.

1.	Rc8	Ra7 +
2.	Kc6	Ra6 +
3.	Kc7	Ra7 +
4.	Kb6	Rd7
5.	Kc6	Ra7
6.	Rc7 +	Rxc7
7.	dxc7	

(1–0)

ENDGAME **203**

W: Kc5, Ra8, Pa6 B: Kg7, Ra1
White moves and wins

Pawn Shelter

White astutely has avoided pushing his pawn to the 7th rank so that his King could shelter in front of the pawn at a7 against checks from Black's Rook. With 1. **Kb6**, White's King steps in to support the pawn, also releasing his Rook for action. Black forcibly takes over the b-file, 1. . . .**Rb1 +**, jamming the King in at a7. Black really has no alternative, for both 1. . . .Kf7, trying to bring his King closer, and 1. . . .Rf1, attempting a flank attack, give White time to activate his Rook, 2. Rc8. After 2. **Ka7 Kf7**, White contests the b-file: 3. **Rb8 Ra1**. Now White can win in several ways. Any safe Rook move down the b-file is acceptable, but the thematic continuation is 4. **Kb7 Rb1 +** 5. **Ka8 Ra1** 6. **a7 Ke7** 7. **Kb7 Rb1 +** 8. **Kc6**, when Black's Rook checks soon terminate and the a-pawn Queens.

1.	**Kb6**	**Rb1 +**	6.	**a7**	**Ke7**
2.	**Ka7**	**Kf7**	7.	**Kb7**	**Rb1 +**
3.	**Rb8**	**Ra1**	8.	**Kc6**	
4.	**Kb7**	**Rb1 +**		(1–0)	
5.	**Ka8**	**Ra1**			

W: Kb2, Rh8 **B:** Kc6, Rh1, Ph3
White moves and draws

Flank Attack

White's King is as well placed as it can be, and in fact cannot stray from b2: 1. Kc2? Kd5   2. Kd2 h2!   3. Ke2 Ra1   4. Rxh2 Ra2+, followed by 5. ...Rxh2. White's Rook, however, can accomplish little on the h-file as long as Black's King has refuge at h2. He needs a flank attack, so White gets going with 1. **Rc8+ Kd5**   2. **Rc3**, keeping the h-pawn in mind along the 3rd rank. Black gets nowhere with 2. ...h2   3. Rh3 (his King has lost his shelter), and 2. ...Rh2+   3. Kb3 signifies zero. But at least his 2. ...Kd4 threatens 3. ...Rb1+, and would eliminate White's Rook. So 3. **Rf3 Ke4**   4. **Rg3 Kf4**   5. **Rc3 Kg4** follows naturally. With the h-pawn now protected by Black's king, White must check: 6. **Rc4+ Kg3**   7. **Rc3+ Kh2**   8. **Rc2+ Kg1**   9. **Rc1+ Kg2**   10. **Rc2+ Kf3**   11. **Rc3+ Ke4**   12. **Rc4+ Kd5.** After 13. **Rc3**, however, Black is back at the starting post. It's a draw.

1. **Rc8+**	**Kd5**	6. **Rc4+**	**Kg3**	11. **Rc3+**	**Ke4**
2. **Rc3**	**Kd4**	7. **Rc3+**	**Kh2**	12. **Rc4+**	**Kd5**
3. **Rf3**	**Ke4**	8. **Rc2+**	**Kg1**	13. **Rc3**	
4. **Rg3**	**Kf4**	9. **Rc1+**	**Kg2**		Draw
5. **Rc3**	**Kg4**	10. **Rc2+**	**Kf3**		

ENDGAME 205

W: Kf1, Rd4 **B:** Kg4, Ra2, Pf4
White moves and draws

Philidor's Draw

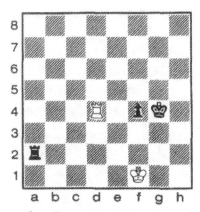

White's King on the Queening square could be driven off, especially now that Black's King and pawn have crossed into White's half of the board. The best way to keep Black's King at bay is for White's Rook to stand guard along the 3rd rank, 1. **Rd3.** Should Black temporize, 1. . . .**Rb2,** White also temporizes by shifting his Rook to any safe square on the 3rd rank, such as 2. **Ra3.** Eventually, to progress, Black must try 2. . . .**f3,** threatening advance to his King to g3. Once the pawn occupies its 6th rank, it can no longer provide shelter in front for its King. The Rook therefore warp-drives to the 8th rank, 3. **Ra8,** menacing checks. If Black then continues 3. . . . .**Kg3,** the game ends in a no-progress draw: 4. **Rg8+ Kf4** 5. **Rf8+ Ke4** 6. **Re8+ Kd4** 7. **Rf8.**

1.	**Rd3**	**Rb2**
2.	**Ra3**	**f3**
3.	**Ra8**	**Kg3**
4.	**Rg8+**	**Kf4**
5.	**Rf8+**	**Ke4**
6.	**Re8+**	**Kd4**
7.	**Rf8**	

(1–0)

ENDGAME **206**

W: Kg1, Rg8 B: Kh4, Ra3, Pg4
White moves and draws

Passive Defense Draws 2

Philidor's drawing position is beyond White because Black's Rook guards the 3rd rank—the place White's Rook needs to be. Meanwhile, Black threatens a serious inroad with 1. . . .Kg3 and 2. . . .Ra1 mate. If White plays 1. Kg2 to stop 1. . . .Kg3, Black forges ahead with 1. . . . Ra2+ and 2. . . .Kg3. White's only chance is to recall his Rook, 1. **Rb8**, so that 1. . . . **Kg3** may be answered by 2. **Rb1**, covering against a mating check along the back rank. True, White's Rook is passively positioned, only capable of moving along the edge, but against a Knight-pawn (or a Rook-pawn) Black cannot take advantage of White's passivity. Even if Black regroups, 2. . . .**Kh3** 3. **Rc1 g3** 4. **Rb1**, he cannot generate serious threats. But Black now plays 4. . . . **Ra2**, shifting his Rook from the 3rd rank to the 2nd. White tempos 5. **Rc1**, and the sequence continues 5. . . .**Rg2+** 6. **Kh1** (not 6. Kf1, because of 6. . . . Kh2) **Rh2+** 7.**Kg1**, and no progress is possible.

1.	**Rb8**	**Kg3**	4. **Rb1**	**Rg2+**
2.	**Rb1**	**Kh3**	5. **Kh1**	**Rh2+**
3.	**Rc1**	**g3**	6. **Kg1**	

Draw

ENDGAME **207**

W: Kb5, Rh6, Pc5 B: Kc8, Rg8
White moves and wins

Passive Defense Loses 2

Passive defense fails against a Bishop-pawn (or Center-pawn).
Black's Rook on g8 offers resistance only on the right of White's
pawn, not on the left, so White inches ahead by 1. **Kb6! Kb8** 2.
c6. If Black tries 2. . . .Ka8 3. Rh7 Rb8+, White squashes
counterplay by 3. Rb7, since 3. . . .Rxb7+ 4. cxb7+ Kb8 5.
Kc6 is a winner. So Black temporizes: 2. . . .**Rf8** 3. **Rh7 Re8**.
But now White is ready for the final push: 4. **Rb7+ Kc8** 5. **Ra7
Kb8** 6. **c7+ Kc8** 7. **Ra8+ Kd7** 8. **Rxe8 Kxe8**. Rooks have
been exchanged, and Black's King is driven from the Queening
square. White finishes with 9. **Kb7 Kd7** 10. **c8/Q+**, and pawn
becomes a Queen on the next move.

1.	Kb6	Kb8		6.	c7+	Kc8
2.	c6	Rf8		7.	Ra8+	Kd7
3.	Rh7	Re8		8.	Rxe8	Kxe8
4.	Rb7+	Kc8		9.	Kb7	Kd7
5.	Ra7	Kb8		10.	c8/Q+	

(1–0)

ENDGAME 208

W: Ka5, Rh7, Pb5 B: Kb8, Rb1
White moves and wins

Driving off the Promotion Square

Black's Rook has lingered too long behind White's a-pawn, and after 1. **Kb6**, it is too late to return to the 8th rank by 1. . . .Rc1 2. Rh8 + Rc8, because White Queens with 3. Rxc8 + Kxc8 4. Ka7, along with 5.b6, 6. b7, and 7. b8/Q. Therefore Black must vacate the Queening square, 1. . . . **Kc8** 2. **Rh8 + Kd7.** The only way to prepare the further advance of the b-pawn is 3. **Rb8!** (Not 3. Ka6 Kc7!). Black cannot prevent the advance, so he tries to keep his King close by: 3. . . . **Rb2** 4. **Ka7 Kc7** 5. **b6 + Kc6** 6. **Rc8 + Kb5** 7. **b7 Ra2 +** 8. **Kb8 Kb6.** White moves on with 9. **Rc1**, threatening 10. Kc8. He can meet 9. . . .Rb2 with 10. Kc8 Ka7, then 11. Ra1 + and 12. b8/Q + . And after 9. . . .**Rh2**, trying for a flank attack, 10. **Rb1 + Kc6** (or 10. . . .Ka6, then 11. Ka8 and 12. b8/Q), White takes the a-file with 11. **Ra1**. At least the finish line is sighted: 11. . . . **Rb2** 12. **Ka8 Rxb7** 13. **Rc1 + Kb6**, 14. **Rb1 + Kc6** 15. **Rxb7.**

1.	Kb6	Kc8	6.	Rc8 +	Kb5	11.	Ra1	Rb2
2.	Rh8 +	Kd7	7.	b7	Ra2 +	12.	Ka8	Rxb7
3.	Rb8	Rb2	8.	Kb8	Kb6	13.	Rc1 +	Kb6
4.	Ka7	Kc7	9.	Rc1	Rh2	14.	Rb1 +	Kc6
5.	b6 +	Kc6	10.	Rb1 +	Kc6	15.	Rxb7	

(1–0)

ENDGAME **209**

W: Kf1, Rf8 **B:** Kf3, Ra2, Pf4
White moves and draws

King to the Short Side

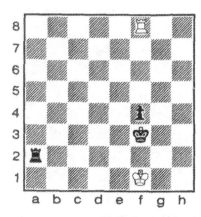

When White cannot set up Philidor's drawing position (the Rook occupying the 3rd rank, preventing the enemy King from approaching), the proper place for the defending Rook against a Bishop-pawn (or a center-pawn) is behind the pawn. The threat of 1. . . .Ra1 mate cannot be met by 1. Re8, as 1. . . .Ra1+ 2. Re1 Rxe1 3. Kxe1 allows the decisive penetration 3. . . .Kg2, and Black's pawn has escort to the Queening square. But by playing his King to the short side of the pawn, 1. **Kg1!**, White keeps alive: 1. . . .**Ra1+** 2. **Kh2 Rf1.** Black's last move is the only feasible way to prepare the advance of his f-pawn, 2. . . .Ke3 being answered by 3. Kg2. However, the lineup of Black pieces on the f-file encourages 3. **Ra8**, threatening a flank attack. Black can try preventive measures with 3. . . .**Re1**, to meet 4. Ra2+ by 4. . . .Re2. But, in that case, White simply returns his Rook to the f-file, 4. **Rf8**, standing watch behind the pawn. The result is a deadlock.

1.	Kg1	Ra1 +
2.	Kh2	Rf1
3.	Ra8	Re1
4.	Rf8	

(1–0)

ENDGAME **210**

W: Kb4, Rc1, Pb5 B: Kd6, Rb8
White moves and wins

Cut-Off—No Checking Distance

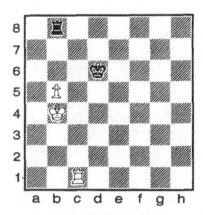

Black's King has been cut off from the Queening file, and his Rook at b8 lacks the requisite three-row checking distance. These two features allow White's King to penetrate quickly and advance his pawn to the 7th rank: 1. **Ka5 Ra8+** 2. **Kb6 Rb8+** 3. **Ka6 Ra8+** 4. **Kb7 Ra2** 5. **b6 Rb2** 6. **Ka7 Ra2+** 7. **Kb8 Kd7** 8. **b7 Ra3.** After 9. **Rd1+ Ke7**, he builds a sheltering bridge for his King, 10. **Rd4.** After the waiting move, 10. . . .**Ra1**, the White King rears from in front of his pawn, 11. **Kc7 Rc1+** 12. **Kb6 Rb1+** 13. **Kc6** (13. Ka6 also wins). It's pointless for Black to check again, 13. . . .**Rb1+**, since White is set up to meet 14. Kb5 Rb1+ with the blocking 15. Rb4. And because White also threatens to transfer the bridge to the 5th rank (14. Rd5), Black tries 13. . . .**Ke6.** This thereby allows 14. **Re4+ Kf6** (or 14. . . .Kf7 15. Re5 and 16. Rb5) 15. **Re8**, supporting the Queening threat while permitting White to escape Black's Rook check via the c- and d-files: 15. . . .**Rc1+** 16. **Kd5 Rd1+** 17. **Kc4 Rc1+** 18. **Kd3 Rd1+** 19. **Kc2** and finis.

1.	Ka5	Ra8+
2.	Kb6	Rb8+
3.	Ka6	Ra8+
4.	Kb7	Ra2
5.	b6	Rb2
6.	Ka7	Ra2+
7.	Kb8	Kd7
8.	b7	Ra3
9.	Rd1+	Ke7
10.	Rd4	Ra1
11.	Kc7	Rc1+
12.	Kb6	Rb1+
13.	Kc6	Ke6
14.	Re4+	Kf6
15.	Re8	Rc1+
16.	Kd5	Rd1+
17.	Kc4	Rc1+
18.	Kd3	Rd1+
19.	Kc2	

(1–0)

ENDGAME **211**

W: Kd2, Rf1 B: Kf5, Re8, Pf4
White moves and draws

Breaking the Barrier

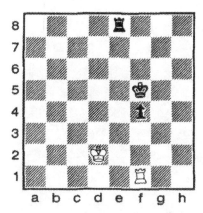

It's a sad business when your King is cut off from the Queening file, as is White's here. An added trouble is that his Rook on f1 lacks the checking distance to halt the Black King's advance. White just manages to contest the e-file, 1. **Re1**, and the Rook exchange by 1. . . .Rxe1 2. Kxe4 enables him to draw the King-and-pawn ending after 2. . . .Kg4 3. Kf2. Black's 1. . . .Re4 doesn't help: 2. Rxe4 Kxe4 3. Ke2 is still a draw. When Black's Rook backs off the f-file, 1. . . .Ra8, White's King does get back to the Queening file, 2. **Ke2 Ra2 +** 3. **Kf3 Ra3 +** 4. **Kf2**. Thus positioned, White can hold out ad nauseam. If for example, Black's King tries to penetrate with 4. . . .Kg4, then 5.**Rg1 +** drives him back to 5. . . .Kf5, after which 6. **Rg8** sets up an endless check from behind.

1.	**Re1**	Ra8
2.	**Ke2**	Ra2 +
3.	**Kf3**	Ra3 +
4.	**Kf2**	Kg4
5.	**Rg1 +**	Kf5
6.	**Rg8**	

Draw

ENDGAME 212

W: Kc3, Rd1, Pc4 B: Kf6, Rc8
White moves and wins

Two-File Cut-Off

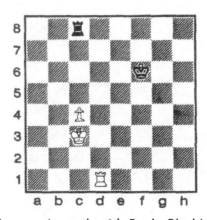

When White's pawn is on the 4th Rank, Black's Rook operates best on its home rank. Three empty ranks separate Rook and pawn, and the Rook can maintain its checking distance. If, however, too many files cut off the defending King from the pawn, even the Black Rook's splendid placement can't garner a draw. There are winning formulas for a pawn on the 4th rank. With a Rook-pawn, the enemy King must be cut off by five files: a Knight-pawn, three files; and Bishop-pawn or a center-pawn, two-files. With a Bishop-pawn on the 4th. White correctly demonstrates by 1. **Re1**, cutting off Black's King by two files. After 1. . . .**Kf5**, he works as close as possible, 2. **Kb4 Rb8+** (Black cannot allow c5) 3. **Ka5 Rc8** 4. **Kb5 Rb8+** 5. **Ka6 Rc8**, before enlisting his Rook to defend his pawn, 6. **Rc1**. Since the c4-c5 advance is inevitable, Black strains his King in, 6. . . .**Ke6**, but too late: 7. **Kb7 Rc5** 8. **Kb6 Rc8** 9. **c5 Kd7** (9. . . .**Rb8+** 10. **Kc7 Rb2** 11. **Rd1** is a standard win for a Bishop-

pawn on the 5th rank needs only a one-file cut-off)   10. c6 +
Kd6   11. Rd1 + Ke7   12. Kb7 Rh8   13. c7, and the c-pawn
holds up the victory banner.

1.	Re1	Kf5
2.	Kb4	Rb8 +
3.	Ka5	Rc8
4.	Kb5	Rb8 +
5.	Ka6	Rc8
6.	Rc1	Ke6
7.	Kb7	Rc5
8.	Kb6	Rc8
9.	c5	Kd7
10.	c6 +	Kd6
11.	Rd1 +	Ke7
12.	Kb7	Rh8
13.	c7	

(1–0)

ENDGAME **213**

W: Kc2, Rh3 B: Kg5, Rh1, Pb4, Ph2
White moves and draws

Active Defense

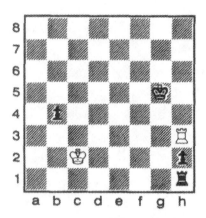

Despite the two-pawn margin, Black cannot win if White defends correctly. His Rook is ill placed, and if White keeps his own Rook on the h-file, the h-pawn can go nowhere. The b4 pawn, moreover, plays no significant role. The only threat is the skewer 1. . . .Ra2 2. Rxh2 Ra2 +. White counters easily with 1. **Kb2.** If Black tries 1. . . .b3, hoping for 2. Kxb3? Rb1 + and 3. . . .h1/Q, White ignores the pawn and waits on the h-file with 2. **Rh8.** To free his Rook for movement, Black's King advances to guard the h-pawn. But after 2. . . .**Kg4** 3. **Rh7 Kg3,** White checks him away, 4. **Rg7 + Kf2,** and then returns to the h-file, 5. **Rh7.** Black can make no progress if White continues this procedure.

	1.	Kb2	b3
	2.	Rh8	Kg4
	3.	Rh7	Kg3
	4.	Rg7 +	Kf2
	5.	Rh7	
		Draw	

ENDGAME **214**

W: Kb2, Ra8, Pa7, Pf5 **B:** Kg7, Ra6
White moves and wins

Skewer

Unlike the previous endgame, in which Black had a worthless
g-pawn, White's f-pawn plays a major role. After 1. f6+, Black
has a dilemma. His Rook can't capture the pawn because that
would give White's Rook the needed tempo to move clear of
a8. Nor can his King take the f-pawn, 1. . . . Kxf6, for that
exposes Black's crown head to a killing check, 1 . . . . Kxf6 2.
Rf8+ and 3. a8/Q. And 1. . . . Kh7 loses to the surging f-pawn,
2. f7, Queening to follow. Finally, blockading the pawn, 1.
. . . Kf7, sets up a winning x-ray (skewer) for White's Rook: 2.
Rh8 Rxa7 3. Rh7+ Kxf6 4. Rxa7.

1. **f6+**   **Kf7**
2. **Rh8**   **Rxa7**
3. **Rh7+**   **Kxf6**
4. **Rxa7**
         (1–0)

ENDGAME **215**

W: Ka6, Rc6, Pb6, Pb5 B: Kb8, Rg8
White moves and wins

Exchanging Down

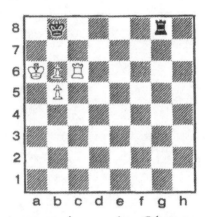

Having two extra pawns is very nice. Often you can give up one in order to reach a position where one extra pawn means victory. This is the guidance behind White's first move, 1. **b7**. Threat of mate at c8 stops Black's Rook from deserting the back rank, so he temporizes with 1. . . .**Rh8**. White follows with 2. **Rc8+** anyway, forcing simplification by 2. . . .**Rxc8** 3. **bxc8/Q+ Kxc8**. Black has regained one of his lost pawns, but faces loss in the resulting King-and-pawn endgame. White continues, 4. **Ka7**, and the b5-pawn can't be stopped from Queening. White's King controls all the squares in front of the b-pawn, including the Queening square, b8.

1.	b7	Rh8
2.	Rc8+	Rxc8
3.	bxc8/Q+	Kxc8
4.	Ka7	

(1–0)

ENDGAME **216**

W: Ka8, Rh7, Pc7 B: Ka5, Rc2, Ph2
White plays and wins

Lasker's Pin

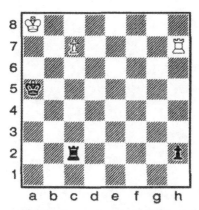

The position appears to be a standoff. Each side has a pawn on respective 7th ranks, ready to Queen. Both Rooks are attacking the enemy's pawn while defending their own. But White can win, thanks to an idea of World Champion Emanuel Lasker (1868–1941). The key piece is White's King, supporting its own pawn, releasing the Rook from its defensive chore. Black's King merely gets in Black's way. White starts with 1. **Kb7**, threatening a new Queen at c8. That forces 1. . . .**Rb2+** 2. **Ka7 Rc2**. Now begins the Lasker maneuver, 3. **Rh5+**, pushing Black's King backward, 3. . . .**Ka4**. The process continues: 4. **Kb7 Rb2+** 5. **Ka6 Rc2** 6. **Rh4+ Ka3**. Black's King has avoided the b-file, keeping it clear for his Rook to give checks. After 7. **Kb6**, White threatens 8. Rxh2 Rxh2 9. c8/Q. Black checks again: 7. . . .**Rb2+** 8. **Ka5! Rc2**. Finally, 9. **Rh3+ Ka2** drives Black's King to the same rank as his Rook. White wins by 10. **Rxh2!**, pinning Black's Rook to his King and ensuring a new Queen: 10. . . .**Rxh2** 11. **c8/Q**.

1. Kb7	Rb2+	5. Ka6	Rc2	9. Rh3+	Ka2
2. Ka7	Rc2	6. Rh4+	Ka3	10. Rxh2	Rxh2
3. Rh5+	Ka4	7. Kb6	Rb2+	11. c8/Q	
4. Kb7	Rb2+	8. Ka5!	Rc2		(1-0)

15

Minor Pieces

ENDGAME 217

W: Kf4, Bb7 **B:** Kg1, Bf1, Ph2
White moves and draws

Stop the Block

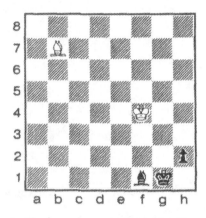

At the moment, Black makes no threat to Queen his pawn, for
1. . . .h1/Q   2. Bxh1 Kxh1 gives King vs. King and Bishop—
drawn because neither player has enough material to checkmate. Black's real charge is 1. . . . Bg2, intercepting the diagonal of White's Bishop so that the pawn can Queen unhindered.
White interferes with 1. **Kg3**, when 1. . . .Bg2 fails to 2. Bxg2.
Black may try to deflect White's Bishop, 1. . . .**Ba6**, for 2. Bxa6
allows Black to Queen. But a simple, safe move along the a8-h1
diagonal, 2. **Bd5**, retains the draw. As long as White's King
remains at g3, Black can't block the line and win.

1. **Kg3**   Ba6
2. **Bd5**
    Draw

W: Kb8,Bf5, Pc7 **B:** Kd6, Ba6
White moves and wins

Deflecting Sacrifice

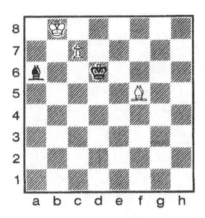

A lone Bishop cannot mate a lone King. White, therefore, must not play 1. c8/Q, because 1. . . .Bxc8   2. Bxc8 is an unwinnable ending. White should concentrate on getting the enemy Bishop off the a6-c8 diagonal. A 1. Bc8 challenge won't do; Black's Bishop just relocates: 1. . . .Bd3   2. Bb7 Bf5, and White is no closer to Queening. But a deflecting sacrifice, 1. **Bd3**, works. Black must accept the sacrifice, 1. . . .**Bxd3**, and White makes his Queen, 2. **c8/Q**. The Queen-vs.-Bishop endgame is an easy win for White, for White's Queen and King move in to deliver mate shortly.

1. **Bd3**   **Bxd3**
2. **c8/Q**
(1–0)

ENDGAME **219**

W: Kc8, Bg3, Pb7 **B:** Kc6, Ba7
White moves and wins

Deflection

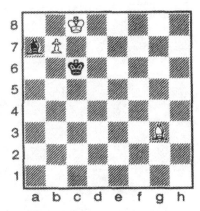

This is a simple deflection. White plays 1. **Bf2** and Black's Bishop has nowhere to go. It must take White's Bishop, 1. . . .**Bxf2**, and White gains a new Queen, 2. **b8/Q**. Mate occurs quickly, for White's pieces can move in on squares opposite in color from the Bishop.

1. **Bf2   Bxf2**
2. **b8/Q**
   (1–0)

ENDGAME **220**

Push-Off 1

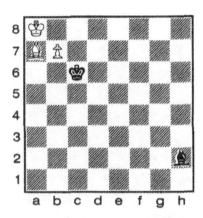

White's efficient win starts with 1. **Bb8**, jabbing Black's Bishop off the h2-b8 diagonal. The exchange of Bishops, 1. . . .Bxb8 2. Kxb8, helps White, for after 2. . . .Kd7 3. Ka7, White promotes the next move. When Black's Bishop leaves the h2-b8 diagonal, 1. . . .**Bg1**, he cannot reposition to stop White from Queening. White merely backs out his Bishop, say 2. **Bg3**, and there goes the b-pawn to Queendom.

1. **Bb8 Bg1**
2. **Bg3**
(1–0)

ENDGAME **221**

Zugzwang 1

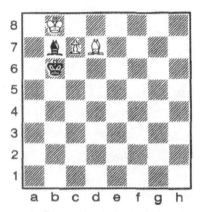

White's victory weapon is found in the rule book: "The two players must move alternately in making one move at a time." White plays his first move, 1. **Bb5,** announcing *zugzwang,* in which any move by Black merely exacerbates his weakened situation. Black cannot stand pat, for the rules says he must move. Any Black Bishop move on the a6-c8 diagonal exposes the Bishop to capture, and any Black Bishop move on the a8-h1 diagonal lets the White pawn be Queened. Any Black King move, say 1. . . .**Kxb5,** unguards Black's Bishop, exposing it to capture by White's King. Once Black's Bishop is gone, White Queens his pawn and flings his hat in the air.

1. **Bb5   Kxb5**
2. **Kxb7**
(1–0)

ENDGAME **222**

W: Kc8, Bd8, Pb7 **B:** Kc6, Bh2
White moves and wins

Centurini's Position

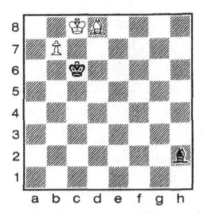

If White can manage to offer a Bishop trade on the b8-h2 diagonal, Black must then redeploy his Bishop to a7, to stem Queening. Then practically any White Bishop move onto the a7-g1 diagonal deflects the Black Bishop at a7, and White Queens his pawn. Easy enough, but it gets harder. How does White challenge the Black Bishop hiding at h2? The winning line begins with 1. **Bh4**, intending 2. Bf2, then 3. Ba7 and 4. Bb8. Black counters with 1. . . .**Kb6** 2. **Bf2+ Ka6**, preventing 3. Ba7. Now comes an ace move, 3. **Bc5!**, luring Black's Bishop out, 3. . . . **Bg3**. White's Bishop aims at c7 by 4. **Be7**, compelling Black's King to retrace his steps: 4. . . .**Kb5** 5. **Bd8+ Kc6**. The position is practically identical to the diagram with one essential difference: the Black Bishop is exposed at g3, rather than safe at h2. White exploits this, gaining a tempo by attacking the Bishop: 6. **Bh4 Bh2** 7. **Bf2 Kb5** 8. **Ba7 Ka6** 9. **Bb8**. This is the

situation White hoped for at the outset. After Black redeploys,
9. . . .Bg1   10. Bg3 Ba7, he falls to the deflection 11. Bf2
Bxf2   12. b8/Q.

1.	Bh4	Kb6
2.	Bf2 +	Ka6
3.	Bc5	Bg3
4.	Be7	Kb6
5.	Bd8 +	Kc6
6.	Bh4	Bh2
7.	Bf2	Kb5
8.	Ba7	Ka6
9.	Bb8	Bg1
10.	Bg3	Ba7
11.	Bf2	Bxf2
12.	b8/Q	

(1–0)

ENDGAME **223**

W: Kb7, Bb8, Pa6 B: Kb5, Be3
White moves and wins

Push-Off 2

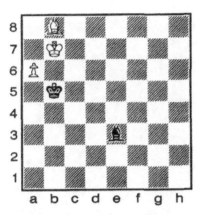

White immediately pressures Black's Bishop off the a7-g1 diagonal by 1. **Ba7**. If Black exchanges Bishops, White Queens the a-pawn in several moves. After 1. . . .**Bf4**, White's Bishop clears out, 2. **Bf2**, letting the pawn advance. Black's Bishop drops back, 2. . . .**Bb8**, defending against the pawn's march. The Bishop, of course, can't be captured with loss of the pawn. White's deflection, 3. **Bg3**, however, ensures Queening for his pawn, since if Black doesn't take White's Bishop, White takes Black's (3. Be1 also wins). In the concluding position, the defensive diagonal a7-b8, containing only two squares, is too short. If it were longer, Black's Bishop might have another place to move while guarding against the pawn's advance.

1.	Ba7	Bf4
2.	Bf2	Bb8
3.	Bg3	Bxg3
4.	a7	

(1–0)

ENDGAME 224

W: Ke7, Bd1 B: Kc3, Bd5, Pb4
White moves and draws

Rear Defense

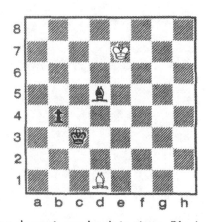

If White's King doesn't get back in time, Black will clear a path for his pawn to Queen. Black's Bishop would play to e4 and then c2, shoving away White's Bishop. His pawn would push to the 7th rank, and only the placing of White's Bishop at a2 would stop the Queening. Black's King steps on a3, and White's Bishop must allow promotion. That's how Black wins in the absence of White's King. But if White's King hies back, he can hold: **1. Kd6 Bb3** (1. . . .Be4 2. Kc5 Bc2 3. Bxc2 Kxc2 4. Kxb4 annihilates any winning changes) **2. Bg4 Kb2** (attempting a *situation where White's Bishop has a shorter defensive diagonal to work with*) **3. Kc5 Ka3 4. Kb6** (not 4. Kb5, for 4. . . .Ba4 + clears the pawn's path with a gain of tempo) **Bf7 5. Bd1 Be8** (threatens White's Bishop by 6. . . .Ba4) **6. Ka5,** and Black cannot force White's Bishop to yield without blocking for one move the advance of the pawn: 6. . . .Bf7 **7. Bc2 Bb3** (blocking his pawn) **8. Bf5 Ba4 9. Be6 Bc2 10. Bf7 Bb1 11.**

Be6 Ba2   12. Bxa2 Kxa2   13. Kxb4. If the defending King can't occupy a safe square against being checked in the pawn's death, an attack on the pawn from behind could save the game.

1.	Kd6	Bb3
2.	Bg4	Kb2
3.	Kc5	Ka3
4.	Kb6	Bf7
5.	Bd1	Be8
6.	Ka5	

Draw

ENDGAME 225

W: Kb6, Bb5, Pa5 B: Kb4, Bc8
White moves and wins

Zugzwang 2

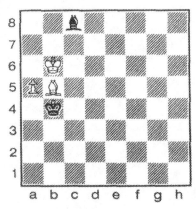

Black's King does attack the pawn from the rear, but once again the defensive diagonal a6–c8 is too short. One more square is needed for Black's Bishop to meet tempo for tempo. After 1. **Bc6**, Black is in *zugzwang*. Either his Bishop must depart the a6–c8 diagonal, allowing the pawn advance, or his King must cease attacking the pawn, granting White a free, safe move to block Black's Bishop with his own. Black's best is 1. . . .**Kc4**, but that fails to 2. **Bb7 Bg4** 3. **a6**, and White's waiting pawn is irrepressible.

1. **Bc6** **Kc4**
2. **Bb7** **Bg4**
3. **a6**
(1–0)

ENDGAME **226**

W: Kf3, Bf1 B: Kd5, Bf6, Pd4, Pe5
White moves and draws

Bishops of Opposite Colors

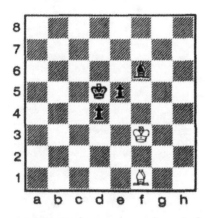

Black has two connected pawns and a dark-square Bishop. White has a light-square Bishop with no pawns, but he can hold the draw. He needs to set up a blockade on the light squares. White's King and Bishop cooperate to guard key light squares (d3 and e4). Black's King can fight for those squares, but he cannot count on aid from his Bishop. It moves on dark squares, unable to control d3 or e4, or to check away White's King. After 1. **Bd3**, White can use the entire b1–h7 diagonal to tempo, whenever he needs to waste a move. If Black ever pushes his e-pawn, White's Bishop gobbles it with impunity, protected by his King. And if Black's King tries to wind around to c3 to guard d3, White's king moves into e4 and his Bishop tempos along the a6–f1 diagonal. There are no winning opportunities for Black.

1. **Bd3**
Draw

ENDGAME **227**

W: Kc1, Bd2 **B:** Ka4, Be4, Pa3, Pb3
White moves and draws

Stopping the Advance

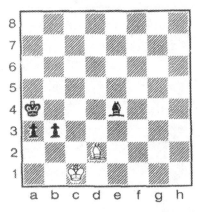

There's menace in Black's passed pawns: they're connected and both lie on the 6th rank. If it were Black's move, he would play 1. . . .b2+, whereupon White would move his King to safety and Black would make a new Queen. But White has hope, because Black has a light-square Bishop while White's Bishop travels only on dark squares. White can set up a two-time guard over b2—a square Black can guard only once. After 1. **Bc3**, Black can never advance his b-pawn, for White would sacrifice his Bishop for Black's two pawns, 1. . . .b2+ 2. Bxb2 axb2 3. Kxb2. Black would lack enough material to mate. If Black instead advances his a-pawn, 1. . . .a2, White's King horns in, 2. Kb2, and progress is impossible.

1. **Bc3**
Draw

ENDGAME **228**

W: Kb5, Bc2, Pb6, Pc6 **B**: Kc8, Bd6
White moves and wins

Outflanking

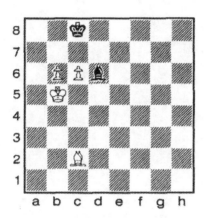

Unlike the previous endgame, here the attacking King (White) can maneuver to either the left or the right of his pawns. He can position himself to protect the c-pawn's advance, from b7 or from d7, depending on where Black's King goes after it is checked, 1. **Bf5 +**. If Black's King heads toward the Kingside, 1. . . .Kd8, White's King sets up at b7: 2. Ka6 Be5   3. Kb7 Bd6   4. c7 + Bxc7   5. bxc7 + Ke7   6. c8/Q. If Black's King answers 1. **Bf5 +** by going Queenside, 1. . . . .Kb8, White's King comes to d7, followed by a pawn push: 2. **Kc4 Bg3**   3. **Kd5 Bf4**   4. **Ke6 Kc8** (4. . . . Be3   5. c7 + Kc8   6. Kd6 +)   5. **Ke7 + Kb8**   6. **Kd7 Bg3**   7. **c7 +**. Bishops of opposite colors often, but not always, produce drawn endgames.

1.	Bf5 +	Kb8
2.	Kc4	Bg3
3.	Kd5	Bf4
4.	Ke6	Kc8
5.	Ke7 +	Kb8
6.	Kd7	Bg3
7.	c7 +	

(1–0)

ENDGAME 229

W: Kc7, Nb7, Pd7 B: Ke7, Nf7
White moves and wins

Deflection

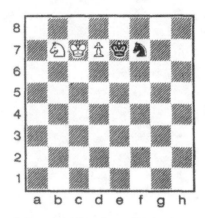

Knights are usefully tricky but have limitations, especially when they play near the board's edge. Here all four pieces guard d8, and Black is willing to sacrifice his Knight for White's d-pawn when it advances. Winning is possible only by deflecting Black's Knight, 1. **Nd6**. Taking White's Knight, 1. . . .**Nxd6** loses immediately to 2. **d8/Q+**. And if Black blocks the pawn, 1. . . .**Nd8**, White answers 2. **Nf5+**, when Black's King is constrained to desert the defense of his Knight. White's King takes the Knight, moves off d8, and the White pawn Queens.

	A	
1.	Nd6	Nxd6
2.	d8/Q+	
	(1–0)	

	B	
1.	Nd6	Nd8
2.	Nf5+	Ke6
3.	Kxd8	
	(1–0)	

W: Ke2, Ng2 B: Kc2, Nc4, Pd2
White moves and draws

Reduction

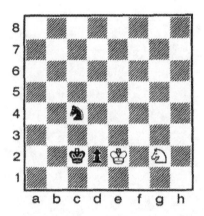

Black is about to Queen at d1. White cannot ankle his Knight to guard d1, for if the Knight moves to e3, he is captured by Black's Knight. The game could be drawn, however, based on Black's inability to expend his pawn for White's knight. White begins 1. Ne1+, and Black can't play 1....dxe1/Q+ because 2. Kxe1 leaves no mating material for either side. Whatever Black plays, White can counter. A sample variation: 1. ...Kc1 2. Nd3+ Kc2 3. Ne1+ Kc3 4. Nf3 (now that Black does not threaten to Queen for at least a move, White can attack Black's pawn) Kc2 5. Nxd2. Though Black wins the Knight, his material is too sparse to win.

1.	Ne1+	Kc1
2.	Nd3+	Kc2
3.	Ne1+	Kc3
4.	Nf3	Kc2
5.	Nxd2	
	Draw	

ENDGAME 231

Corralling 1

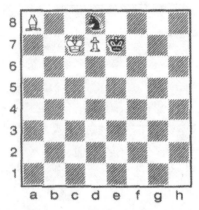

A Bishop can ruin a defending Knight's day. After 1. **Bd5**, Black is in *zugzwang*. If he moves his King, his Knight goes down for nothing. If he moves his Knight anywhere, White's Bishop captures, and White proclaims a new Queen on the next move. Note how the Bishop from d5 guards all the squares open to the Knight: b7, c6, e6, and f7. The Bishop is said to "corral" the knight, and this corralling talent contributes to its general superiority over a Knight in the endgame.

1. **Bd5**　　**Nf7**
2. **Bxf7**　　**Kxf7**
3. **d8/Q**
　　(1–0)

W: Kg3, Bf7, Pg6 **B:** Kh8, Ng7
White moves and wins

Encirclement

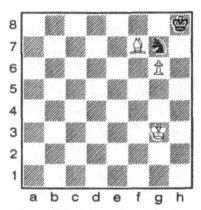

Black's pieces are placed terribly. After 1. **Kg4**, Black must make a move that loses his Knight. His King can't move and the Knight's only squares (e8, e6, f5, and h5) are all guarded by White's Pieces. Once White has captured the impotent horse, winning depends simply on not stalemating the Black King. White proceeds carefully, promoting his pawn to mate. A number of other variations win equally well.

1.	**Kg4**	**Ne6**
2.	**Bxe6**	**Kg7**
3.	**Kg5**	**Kh8**
4.	**Bd7**	**Kg7**
5.	**Kf5**	**Kg8**
6.	**Kf6**	**Kh8**
7.	**g7+**	**Kh7**
8.	**Be6**	**Kh6**
9.	**g8/Q**	**Kh5**
10.	**Qh8**	**mate**

(1–0)

ENDGAME **233**

W: Ke7, Bf3, Pd6 B: Kc5, Nf8
White moves and wins

Zugzwang 3

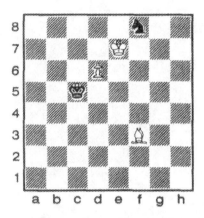

Black's clumsy Knight gets corralled after 1. **Be4**. Black's King could attack White's Bishop, 1. . . .**Kd4**, but this releases White's pawn from attack. White has a safe move to capture Black's Knight, and a new White Queen stands up. Black has been *zugzwang*ed.

1. **Be4**   **Kd4**
2. **Kxf8**   **Kxe4**
3. **d7**

(1–0)

ENDGAME **234**

W: Kd3, Ng2 **B:** Kb3, Bc5, Pc3
White moves and draws

Blockade

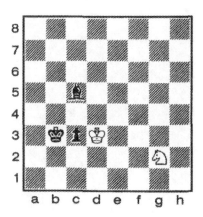

Black's pawn and a strong Bishop face a weak Knight. But the old shoe for White works: 1. Ne1 (preventing the pawn's movement) **Bf2** 2. **Nc2 Bb6** 3. **Ne1 Bc5** 4. **Nc2 Bf2** (trying to *zugzwang* the Knight) 5. **Na3**, and White holds. Black's King can't capture the Knight because it would lose his pawn. The pawn must remain on board to make a new Queen, but Black has no safe way to advance it. White's pesky Knight is just resourceful enough to maintain the blockade.

1.	**Ne1**	**Bf2**
2.	**Nc2**	**Bb6**
3.	**Ne1**	**Bc5**
4.	**Nc2**	**Bf2**
5.	**Na3**	
	Draw	

ENDGAME **235**

W: Kg8, Ba2, Pb2 **B:** Ke1, Na5
White moves and wins

Corralling 2

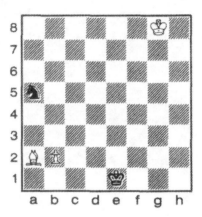

A Knight on the rim is dim, regardless of which rim. Here White's corral, 1. **Bd5**, is devastating. The Bishop traps the Knight, and after 1. . . . **Kd2**, the pawn shags it, 2. **b4**. Black ought to divert the Bishop, 2. . . . **Nb7** 3. **Bxb7**, to give his King time to get back in the action, 3. . . . **Kc3**. But once the pawn is safe from capture, 4. **b5 Kb4** 5. **Ba6**, White has time to burn to bring his King toward Queenside as an escort for the promoting pawn.

1. **Bd5**	**Kd2**	7. **Ke7**	**Kc7**
2. **b4**	**Nb7**	8. **Ke8**	**Kb8**
3. **Bxb7**	**Kc3**	9. **Kd8**	**Ka8**
4. **b5**	**Kb4**	10. **Kc7**	**Ka7**
5. **Ba6**	**Kc5**	11. **Bc8**	**Ka8**
6. **Kf7**	**Kb6**	12. **Bb7 +**	**Ka7**
		13. **b6**	**mate**

(1–0)

W: Kd1, Bd4 **B:** Kb1, Na4, Pa2
White moves and draws

Corner Retreat

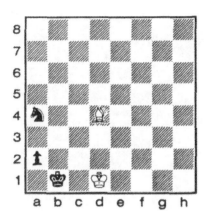

White looks to sacrifice his Bishop for Black's pawn, once the pawn advances to a1. But Black plans to thwart that by interposing his Knight at b2, blocking the Bishop. With no time to spare, White must play 1. **Ba1!**. If Black captures the Bishop, White draws by moving his King to c2, which is the same color square as that occupied by Black's Knight. This traps Black's King, and his Knight is unable to reposition in order to drive away White's king. If Black instead answers by inserting 1. . . .**Nb2 +**, White plays 2. **Kd2**. After 2. . . .**Nc4 +**, since Black's Knight is now on a dark square, White's King also makes to a dark square, 3. **Kd1 Kxa1**, trapping Black's King in the corner. Black's moves no longer matter. White draws by moving his King back and forth between c2 and c1.

1.	**Ba1**	**Nb2 +**		7.	**Kc1**	**Ne2 +**
2.	**Kd2**	**Nc4 +**		8.	**Kc2**	**Nd4 +**
3.	**Kd1**	**Kxa1**		9.	**Kc1**	**Nb3 +**
4.	**Kc2**	**Ne3 +**		10.	**Kc2**	**Nd2**
5.	**Kc1**	**Nd1**		11.	**Kc1**	
6.	**Kc2**	**Nc3**			Draw	

ENDGAME 237

W: Kb7, Nd4, Pd7 B: Kd3, Ba5
White moves and wins

Driving Off

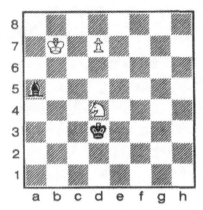

Whatever its drawbacks in endgames, don't sell a knight short. After 1. Nc6, Black's Bishop is attacked and has no safe place to move and still prevent the Queening of White's pawn. If it goes to b6 or c7, it's taken by White's King. If it goes to d8, the Knight becomes the gobbler. And if it retreats along the a5-e1 diagonal, White Queens it pawn.

1. Nc6
(1–0)

W: Kb5, Nc8, Pa6 **B:** Kd5, Bd4
White moves and wins

Block Out

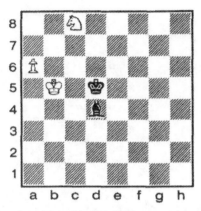

White's Knight shuts out Black's Bishop with 1. **Nb6 +**. Whether Black then takes the Knight, 1. . . .**Bxb6** 2. **Kxb6**, or moves his King out of check. White pushes his a-pawn to Queen. Mate soon follows.

1.	Nb6 +	Bxb6
2.	Kxb6	Kd6
3.	a7	

(1–0)

W: Kd5, Ne4, Pc5 B: Kh1, Bh2
White moves and wins

Convoy

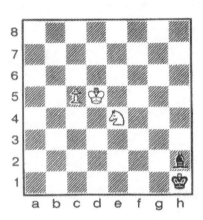

If the Black King were closer, it could shoulder some of the defensive chores and the game would draw. But after 1. **Nd6**, the beleaguered Bishop is exiled from the proceedings, and White leans on Queening shortly. Black tries to relocate his Bishop along the a5-d8 diagonal: 1. . . .**Bg1** 2. **c6 Bb6**. Although the pawn is momentarily stopped, Black's King is so removed that White has time-plus to get his pieces to the right squares to shoo the Bishop: 3. **Ke6 Bc7** 4. **Kd7 Bb8** 5. **Ne8 Kg2** 6. **Nc7 Ba7** 7. **Na6 Bb6** 8. **Nc5 Kf3** 9. **Na4 Ba5** 10. **Nb2 Ke4** 11. **Nc4**, The Bishop must clear out, permitting a triumphant coronation.

1.	Nd6	Bg1	7.	Na6	Bb6
2.	c6	Bb6	8.	Nc5	Kf3
3.	Ke6	Bc7	9.	Na4	Ba5
4.	Kd7	Bb8	10.	Nb2	Ke4
5.	Ne8	Kg2	11.	Nc4	
6.	Nc7	Ba7		(1–0)	

Glossary

The following terms relate technically to the endgames in the text, and may or may not also be standard English usage. The glossary entries are designed to assist your reading of the book and your understanding of chess.

ACTIVE *(adj.)*   Refers to a dynamic move or placement.

ANALYSIS *(n.)*   The process of determining, through careful examination, the best moves in a variation or position.

ATTACK *(n.)*   A threat to capture an enemy piece. A force aimed at a specific objective or for a definite purpose.

BACK-ROW MATE *(n.)*   A checkmate given by a Queen or Rook along the board's edge. Also called a Back-Rank Mate.

BACKWARD PAWN *(n.)*   A weak pawn that has fallen behind friendly pawns which cannot protect it.

BAD BISHOP *(n.)*   A passive Bishop, often obstructed by its own pawns; usually a permanent disadvantage.

BARRIER *(n.)*   A vertical or horizontal row of squares, generally controlled by a Rook, that the enemy King cannot cross.

BASIC MATE *(n.)*   A checkmate that can be forced with pure, elemental combinations of pieces (no pawns) against a lone enemy King. The four standard checkmates are King and Queen; King and Rook; King and two bishops; and King, Bishop, and Knight. Other basic mates include Queen and Rook, and two Rooks.

BEHIND A PASSED PAWN *(adv.)*   Generally used to describe the best place for a Rook to station itself when attacking an advancing pawn. As the pawn advances up the board, the Rook's mobility increases.

BISHOPS OF OPPOSITE COLORS *(n.)*   A situation in which each player has only one Bishop—one traveling on light squares, the other on dark. They can never attack each other or guard the same squares. Also called Opposite-Color Bishops.

BLIND SIDE *(n.)* The side of the board away from the protected passed pawn or attacking zone, in situations where Kings and pawns confront each other over an extended area. The live side is the closer one.

BLOCKADE *(n.)* A defensive strategy that consists of preventing the advance of an enemy pawn (usually a passed pawn) by occupying and/or guarding the square in front of it.

BP *(n.)* The abbreviation for Bishop-pawn, a pawn on either the c- or f-file.

BREAKTHROUGH *(n.)* A pawn sacrifice whose purpose is to open lines and/or to create a passed pawn.

BRIDGE *(n.)* A blocking move (usually by a Rook) that stops enemy Rook-checks.

BUILDING A BRIDGE *(n.)* In Rook endings, when the stronger side has a pawn on the 7th rank, he prepares to block enemy Rook-checks by positioning his own Rook on its 4th rank (or occasionally, its 5th or 6th rank). The term was created by Aron Nimzovich (1886–1935). See LUCENA'S POSITION.

CANDIDATE *(n.)* The pawn likely to be passed. Also called the Candidate Passed Pawn. Usually, it is a pawn with no enemy pawn in front of it on the same file.

CAPABLANCA'S RULE *(n.)* A principle that determines which pawn to move first when pushing a group of pawns. The player should start by advancing the unopposed pawn (candidate pawn), as illustrated by Jose Raoul Capablanca in several of his books.

CENTRALIZE *(v.)* To place one's pieces in, or as close to, the board's center (e4, d4, e5, d5). So placed, they have more scope and can limit their enemy counterparts.

CENTURINI'S POSITION *(n.)* A famous endgame of King, Bishop, and Knight-pawn vs. King and Bishop, in which an elaborate Bishop maneuver gains a tempo and wins.

CHECKING DISTANCE *(n.)* The minimum distance a Rook needs to thwart an enemy passed pawn's advance and/or harass the enemy King, without fear of attack itself. The Rook, a long-range piece, functions to best advantage when it is at least three squares away from its target (the enemy King or pawn). Thus, if White's King were on d4 and his pawn on e4, while Black's Rook checked from d8, the three squares between ensure that the Rook has the "checking distance" and could prevent the advance of King and pawn. If the Rook were at d7, however, with only two squares between, the Rook would have no "checking distance," and White's King could approach, subsequently escaping checks and advancing his pawn.

COMPANION SQUARE *(n.)*   Another name for a CORRESPONDING SQUARE.

CONJUGATE SQUARE *(n.)*   Another name for a CORRESPONDING SQUARE.

CONNECTED PASSED PAWNS *(n.)*   Two friendly passed pawns on adjacent files, which can protect each other.

COORDINATE SQUARE *(n.)*   Another name for a CORRESPONDING SQUARE.

CORRALLING A KNIGHT *(n.)*   Trapping a Knight with a Bishop along the edge of the board. For example, a Black Knight on a5 is corralled by a White Bishop on d5.

CORRESPONDING SQUARE *(n.)*   A square accessible only to one King that correlates to a square accessible only to the other. In this complex oppositional relationship, in which pawns are obstacles, preferably one's King should occupy its corresponding square immediately after the opponent's King occupies its. Usually referred to in the plural, "corresponding squares." Also called Companion Square, Conjugate Square, Coordinate Square, Related Square, and Sister Square.

CP *(n.)*   The abbreviation for center-pawn, a pawn on either the d- or e-file.

CRITICAL SQUARE *(n.)*   A square whose occupation by the superior King ensures success of a task. If a player has a King and pawn and his opponent has only a King, he wins if his King can occupy any of his pawn's critical squares. Rook-pawns have only one critical square, while other passed pawns have three. Fixed pawns may have as many as six.

CROSS-CHECK *(n.)*   A check that blocks the enemy's previous check. Especially valuable as a tactic in Queen endings to thwart perpetual attack from the opposing Queen.

CROSSOVER *(n.)*   A maneuver by a King in front of and across its passed pawn to reach the outside critical square. Also called the Overpass, distinguishing it from the Underpass.

CUT-OFF *(n.)*   Creation of a barrier with a Queen or Rook, which prevents the enemy King from escaping across a rank or file or from participating.

DARK-SQUARE BISHOP *(n.)*   A Bishop that travels only on dark squares. For White, the Bishop that starts the game on c1; for Black, the one that begins on f8.

DECOY *(n.)*   An outside passed pawn offered as a sacrifice to lure an enemy piece (usually the King) from the main battle.

DIAGONAL MARCH *(n.)*   A maneuver enabling a King to approach two squares in opposite directions simultaneously by traveling along a diagonal that is equidistant from both.

DIAGONAL OPPOSITION *(n.)*   An opposition in which the Kings are separated by one, three, or five-squares along the same diagonal. It includes diagonal opposition (one square in between), distant diagonal opposition (three squares in between), and long-distant diagonal opposition (five squares in between). See OPPOSITION.

DIRECT OPPOSITION *(n.)*   An opposition on a file, rank, or diagonal in which the Kings are separated by one square. Direct vertical opposition is along a file, direct horizontal opposition is along a rank, and direct diagonal opposition is along a diagonal. See OPPOSITION.

DISTANT OPPOSITION *(n.)*   An opposition on a file, rank, or diagonal in which the Kings are separated by three squares. Distant horizontal opposition is along a file, distant vertical opposition is along a rank, and distant diagonal opposition is along a diagonal. See OPPOSITION.

DISCOVERED ATTACK *(n.)*   With this tactic, one moves a piece, unveiling another friendly piece's line of power. When both the moving and stationary pieces give simultaneous threats, it is a double attack. Also called Discovery.

DOUBLE ATTACK *(n.)* A simultaneous attack against two separate targets, either by one piece against two (a fork), or by two pieces menacing different threats (such as a discovery).

DOUBLED PAWNS *(n.)* Two friendly pawns that line up on the same file and can't protect each other.

DOWN THE EXCHANGE *(adv.)* Having a Knight or Bishop against an enemy Rook. See UP THE EXCHANGE.

DRAW BY REPETITION *(n.)* See REPETITION OF POSITION RULE.

EDGE *(n.)* The board's four outside rows of squares: a-file, h-file, 1st rank, and 8th rank.

EXCHANGE *(n.)* The swapping of a Rook for a minor piece (Bishop or Knight). You either "win the exchange" or "lose the exchange."

FEINT *(n.)* A King maneuver, in which a player threatens to perform an action which gains time so that he can really do something else.

FIFTY-MOVE RULE *(n.)* A law of chess that permits a player to claim a draw if fifty moves have been played without a piece having been exchanged or a pawn moved.

FIXED PAWNS *(n.)* Two pawns—one White, one Black—facing and blocking each other along the same file, so that neither can move.

FLANK ATTACK *(n.)* A Rook attack against the enemy King from the side of a passed pawn, as opposed to an attack against the enemy pawn and King from behind or in front. When effective rear attacks are impossible, this may be the only way to save a game.

FLIGHT SQUARE *(n.)* A place for the King to flee, avoiding back-row mates and other threats. See LUFT.

FRONTAL ATTACK *(n.)* A direct attack, usually by a Rook on a passed pawn, along the file of squares in front of the pawn, as opposed to a rear attack from behind. Kings also give frontal attacks, especially by setting up blockades. See REAR ATTACK.

FRONTIER *(n.)* An imaginary line separating the 4th and 5th ranks; a term coined by Aron Nimzovich.

GAIN A MOVE *(v.)* To complete an action, sequence, or plan in one less move than apparently needed. A player gains advantage by causing or forcing his opponent to waste a move, usually a response to a threat. Also called Gain a Tempo.

HOLE *(n.)* A weakness, usually a square on one's 3rd rank which is incapable of being defended by a pawn.

HORIZONTAL OPPOSITION *(n.)* An opposition in which the Kings line up on the same rank, separated by one, three, or five squares. Direct horizontal opposition has one square between, distant horizontal opposition has three squares between, and long-distant horizontal opposition has five squares between. See OPPOSITION.

INSUFFICIENT MATING MATERIAL *(n.)* The state of being in a drawn position because neither side has enough material left to force mate as, for example, when only two Kings remain or when one side has a lone Bishop or Knight.

ISOLATED PAWN *(n.)* A pawn with no friendly pawns on either adjacent file and which therefore cannot be guarded by another pawn.

KEY SQUARE *(n.)* Another name for CRITICAL SQUARE.

KING-BISHOP *(n.)* For either side, the Bishop that starts the game on the Kingside (f1 for White, f8 for Black).

KNIGHT'S CORRALL *(n.)* A Bishop trap of a Knight along the edge.

KNIGHT'S JUMP *(n.)* A unit of distance based on how the Knight moves. If square *a* is a Knight's jump away from square *b*, it means a Knight sitting on *a* could move to *b*. Also called a Knight's Move.

KNIGHT'S-MOVE OPPOSITION *(n.)* An opposition in which the Kings do not occupy the same row or sit on squares of the same color. They stand in opposition, even though they are a Knight's jump away from each other, because blocked pawns prevent the Kings from assuming typical oppositional distances. Thus, different rules apply.

LIGHT PIECES *(n.)* Bishops and Knights. Also called Minor Pieces.

LIGHT-SQUARE BISHOP *(n.)* A Bishop that travels on light squares only. For White, the Bishop that starts the game on f1; for Black, the one that begins on c8.

LIVE SIDE *(n.)* The side of the board closest to the protected passed pawn or attacking zone when Kings and pawns confront each other over an extended area. The blind side is the more distant one.

LONG-DISTANT OPPOSITION *(n.)* An opposition along a file, rank, or diagonal in which the Kings are separated by five squares. Long-distant vertical opposition is along a file, long-distant horizontal opposition is along a rank, and long-distant diagonal opposition is along a diagonal. See OPPOSITION.

LONG SIDE *(n.)* For Knight, Bishop, and center-pawns, the side that offers the greatest number of files leading to the edge of the board. The concept is especially important in Rook endgames, in which the Rook must be far away in order to give a successful flank attack. Thus, the principle "Move your Rook to the long side."

LOSE A MOVE *(v.)* To create a *zugzwang* situation by a series of moves that force the opponent to give way. It involves keeping the same position, but transferring the move to the opponent. Also called Lose a Tempo.

LUCENA'S POSITION *(n.)* Named after Luis Ramirez Lucena (fifteenth–sixteenth century), an important position in the King, Rook, and pawn on the 7th rank vs. King and Rook endgame. It involves escaping the pesky checks of the enemy Rook by creating shelter for the harassed King. The technique is "building a bridge"—placing one's Rook first on its 4th rank. See BRIDGE.

LUFT *(n.)* A German term meaning "air" or, figuratively, breathing space. A flight square created for a King by moving a pawn in front of the King so that it can escape back-row mates.

MAJOR PIECES *(n.)* Queens and Rooks. Also called Heavy Pieces.

MANEUVER *(n.)* A redeployment or a series of moves, usually not involving checks or exchanges, designed to improve the placement of one or more pieces.

MINOR PIECES *(n.)* Bishops and Knights. Also called Light Pieces.

NP *(n.)* The abbreviation for Knight-pawn, a pawn on either the g- or b-file.

OBLIQUE OPPOSITION *(n.)* Another name for RECTANGULAR OPPOSITION.

OCCUPATION *(n.)* Direct placement of a piece or pawn on a specific square.

OPEN FILE *(n.)* A vertical row of eight squares (such as d1 through d8), devoid of pawns. A line especially effective for Rooks.

OPPOSITE-COLOR BISHOPS *(n.)* See BISHOPS OF OPPOSITE COLORS.

OPPOSITION *(n.)* A *Zugzwang* relationship between the Kings, depending mainly on the distance separating them. If the Kings "stand in opposition," whichever moves is at a disadvantage and must give ground. The Kings use opposition in their fight over a passed pawn's critical squares. The attacking King "takes the opposition" trying to occupy a critical square, and the defending King "takes the opposition" to prevent the enemy King from occupying that critical square or others. In standard oppositions (vertical, horizontal, or diagonal; and direct, distant, and long-distant), the Kings occupy squares of the same color and are separated by an odd number of squares (one, three, or five) along the same row (file, rank, or diagonal).

OPPOSITIONAL FIELD *(n.)* The interrelation of every possible opposition, taken in sequence, extending across the entire board. Thus, if a player gets the long-distant opposition, he can convert it to a distant opposition as the opponent's King approaches, and thereafter to a direct opposition if his King steps even closer. See OPPOSITION.

OUTFLANKING *(n.)* An invasion by the King from the flank, usually relying on the opposition and often to occupy an outside critical square, especially to win a fixed enemy pawn defended only by its King.

OUTSIDE CRITICAL SQUARE *(n.)* The critical square farthest from the enemy King. It is generally the hardest critical square for the enemy King to defend. See UNDERPASS and CROSSOVER.

OUTSIDE PASSED PAWN *(n.)* A pawn free to move toward promotion, positioned away from the main fighting area. It is typically used to decoy the enemy King to one side of the board (by threatening to become a new Queen), so that the friendly King can triumph on the other side.

OVERPASS *(n.)* Another name for crossover.

PASSIVE *(adj.)* Refers to a move that merely guards or wards off, with no element of counterplay. An example is a passive Rook's defense, which generally is played to stop mate along the board's edge.

PASSED PAWN *(n.)* A pawn free to move to its promotion square, with no enemy pawns to block its progress to the last rank.

PAWN ISLAND *(n.)* A group of friendly pawns separated from other friendly pawns by at least one file. The fewer pawn islands a player has, the better.

PAWN MAJORITY *(n.)* A group of pawns in one area that outnumber the enemy pawns opposing them. If a player has a healthy pawn majority, he can create a passed pawn. When both Kings castle Kingside and a player has a Queenside majority, he can produce a passed pawn and use it as a decoy to lure the enemy King from the Kingside, leaving that sector defenseless. See QUEENS MAJORITY.

PERPETUAL CHECK *(n.)* A sequence of checks from which the enemy King cannot esape, but cannot be mated, either. This technique is used by the checking side to draw the game by repetition of position. As a player is about to repeat a position for the third time, the rules allow him to claim a draw. The repetitions need not occur on consecutive moves for the rule to apply. Also called Perpetual and Perpetual Attack.

PHILIDOR'S DRAW *(n.)* In situations of King, Rook, and pawn vs. King and Rook, cutting off the approaching King by establishing one's Rook on its 3rd rank, with one's own King standing in the path of the enemy pawn. A player can draw by shifting his Rook along the 3rd rank, preventing the attacking King from coming closer. If the player's opponent pushes the pawn to block out the Rook and break the cut-off, allowing the King to advance, the draw can be maintained by transferring the Rook to the back rank, where it can threaten to give an annoying series of checks.

PHILIDOR'S POSITION *(n.)* In the King, Rook, and Bishop vs. King and Rook endgame, a winning position correctly analyzed by Francois-Andres Danican Philidor (1726–95).

POSITIONAL DRAW *(n.)* A drawn situation in which the poor placement of otherwise winning material, and/or the excellent positions of the enemy defenders, prevents the game from being won. An example is King, Bishop, and Rook-pawn vs. King, when the Bishop is unable to drive the enemy King from the promotion square.

PROMOTION SQUARE *(n.)* The square on a passed pawn's 8th rank that the pawn must occupy to become a new piece. Also called the Queening Square.

PROTECTED PASSED PAWN *(n.)* A pawn guarded by a friendly pawn, therefore safe from enemy King attack.

PROMOTION *(n.)* Creation of a new Queen when a pawn reaches its last rank. Also called Queening.

QUEEN-BISHOP *(n.)* For either side, the Bishop that starts the game on the Queenside (c1 for White, c8 for Black).

QUEENING SQUARE *(n.)* Another name for Promotion Square.

QUEENSIDE MAJORITY *(n.)* An advantage in which having more pawns on the Queenside than the opponent enables one to create a passed pawn that may be used as a decoy.

REAR ATTACK *(n.)* An attack by a King or Rook from behind a passed pawn. This is generally the most powerful posting for a Rook. Though the King tends to be better placed defensively in front of an advancing pawn, thereby blockading it, sometimes a game can be saved by menacing the pawn with the King from the rear.

RELATED SQUARE *(n.)* Another name for CORRESPONDING SQUARE.

RECTANGULAR OPPOSITION *(n.)* An opposition in which the Kings do not oppose each other along the same rank, file, or diagonal, but do occupy squares of the same color. If a rectangle were drawn along the perimeter of squares containing the two Kings, and if both the long and short sides of the rectangle contain an odd number of squares, the Kings stand in "rectangular opposition," whereby it is undesirable for either King to move. It is also called Oblique Opposition. For example, if White's King were on c2 and Black's King were on e6, the Kings would then be in rectangular opposition, and whichever one moves is at a disadvantage. See OPPOSITION.

REPETITION OF POSITION RULE *(n.)*   A rule of the game whereby as a player is about to create a position that has already occurred twice, though not necessarily on consecutive moves, he is permitted to claim a draw. This rule is usually invoked or sought by the inferior side to avert defeat. Also known as Draw By Repetition.

RIGHT-TRIANGLE CHECK *(n.)*   An imagined right triangle that can be traced over the arrangement of three pieces (two Kings in the same rank or file, separated by one square, and one checking major piece, placed at a right angle to the line of Kings). If the Kings are on a file, the major piece checks along a rank. If on a rank, the check comes from along the file. In all cases, a right-triangle check drives the enemy King back a row. Along the board's edge, such a check gives mate.

ROLL *(n.)*   A sequence of forcing checks by two pieces of like power that drive a defending King to the edge or corner, row after row, by consecutive files, ranks, or diagonals.

RP *(n.)*   The abbreviation for Rook-pawn, a pawn on either the a- or h-file.

SEVENTH RANK *(n.)*   Generally, an important rank for an invading Rook to occupy. Along the 7th rank, an aggressive Rook may confine the enemy King, set up mating threats, and often attack a number of pawns.

SHORT SIDE *(n.)*   The side of a Knight, Bishop, or center-pawn offering the fewest number of files to the edge of the board. (Rook-pawns have only one side). Ideally, the defender tries to position his King on the short side of a passed pawn so that he keeps the long side clear for Rook-checks. Thus, if a player's

King must defend itself by moving to the short or long side of a Bishop or center-pawn, the principle says "Move to the short side."

SIMPLIFY *(v.)* To exchange pieces and reduce complications.

SISTER SQUARES *(n.)* Another name for CORRESPONDING SQUARES.

SKEWER *(n.)* A tactic by which a piece is forced to move out of the way, exposing another piece or pawn to capture. The two most important types of endgame skewers are those from Queen to enemy King and Queen, and Rook to enemy King and Rook. Also called x-ray.

SQUARE OF THE PAWN *(n.)* A visual trick to determine if a King can overtake a passed pawn. You envision a group of squares as a square block, where the sides of the block are equal in length to the number of ordinary chessboard squares extending from a passed pawn to its Queening square. If, on the move, the defending King can play to an ordinary chessboard square within the imagined block known as "the square of the pawn," the King can overtake the pawn and prevent it from Queening. If the King can't move within the "square of the pawn," the pawn becomes a new Queen. If a passed pawn occupies a6, the "square of the pawn" is a three by three block containing nine regular squares, including a6, a7, a8, b8, c8, c7, c6, b6, and b7. If the pawn is on a5, the "square" contains 16 regular squares, with boundaries running from a5 to a8 to d8 to d5. On a4 the square houses twenty-five small squares, going from a4 to a8 to e8 to e4. On a3 the square consists of thirty-six regular squares, reaching from a3 to a8 to f8 to f4. If a passed pawn sits on a2, because of its ability to move two squares ahead on its first move, you should pretend it's really on a3 for the purpose of determining its square, which therefore extends from a3 to a8 to f8 to f4. The "square of the pawn" is also referred to as a Quadrant or Quadrangle.

SQUEEZE *(n.)* A *zugzwang* in King and pawn versus King endings that forces the inferior King to move off the promotion square, leading to the pawn's Queening. It occurs when the pawn safely advances to the 7th rank without giving check. Some writers distinguish between squeeze and *zugzwang*. For them, *zugzwang* means neither player wants to move, while squeeze means only one player doesn't want to move. I do not use the term the latter way, here or anywhere else.

STALEMATE *(n.)*   A draw because the player on the move, not already in check, has no legal move. The rules of the game make this situation a draw. If you are losing, one resource is to find a way to sacrifice your remaining material, leaving yourself in stalemate, without a legal play.

SUPPORT MATE *(n.)*   A checkmate given by a Queen on an adjacent square to the enemy King. The Queen must be guarded by a friendly piece or pawn.

TAKING AWAY THE LAST SQUARE *(n.)*   Reducing the territory available to a lone King by seizing control of the square it previously occupied. A tactic used to drive a King toward the edge or corner.

TAKING THE OPPOSITION *(n.)*   Getting the advantage for your King by moving it to oppose the enemy King along the same file, rank, or diagonal, leaving one, three, or five squares between. The enemy King, occupying a square of the same color, then or soon, has to give way. Also moving your King into position with the enemy King to shape a rectangle, as in rectangular opposition, where both the long and short sides of the rectangle are odd. See OPPOSITION.

TEMPO *(n.)*   A unit of time represented by one move.

THEORY OF CORRESPONDING SQUARES *(n.)*   A profoundly comprehensive theory attempting to explain all endgames with just Kings and unmovable pawns, drawing on elaborate calculations, complex analyses, numerous practical examples, and abstruse formulas.

THREAT *(n.)*   An attempt to gain advantage by trapping, capturing, and/or influencing the enemy King, hostile forces, and/or squares.

TRIANGULATION *(n.)*   A maneuver in which a King (and rarely the Queen) takes two moves to occupy a square it could have reached in one. It is usually done to lose a move, placing the other side in *zugzwang*. While executing this maneuver, the King's movement traces a triangle.

TWO BISHOPS *(n.)* A type of advantage, whereby one side has two Bishops and the other has a Bishop and Knight, or two Knights.

UNDERPROMOTION *(n.)* Creation of a Rook, Bishop, or Knight—instead of a Queen—when a pawn reaches its 8th rank.

UNIVERSE *(n.)* For a passed pawn, an imagined section of the board consisting of three files: the file the pawn occupies and the adjacent files to the immediate left and right. When a King and pawn face a lone King, the fight to promote the pawn generally is confined within this zone.

UP THE EXCHANGE *(adv.)* Having the advantage of a Rook against a minor piece (Bishop or Knight).

VERTICAL OPPOSITION *(n.)* An opposition in which the Kings line up on the same file, separated by one, three, or five squares. Direct vertical opposition has one square between, distant vertical opposition has three squares between, and long-distant vertical opposition has five squares between. See OPPOSITION.

WAITING MOVE *(n.)* A move that shifts the turn to one's opponent without changing anything important in the position, often accomplished by moving a piece one square, ahead or behind, along the line it already occupies.

WEAKNESS *(n.)* A square or pawn that no friendly pawn can protect.

WRONG BISHOP *(n.)* In situations of King, Bishop, and Rook-pawn vs. a lone King, a Bishop that travels on squares of different color from the Rook-pawn's promotion square. Thus, it cannot drive the enemy King from the corner and the game is drawn. In situations of King and Rook vs. King and Bishop, a Bishop that is unable to occupy the squares horizontally or vertically adjacent to the corner. Thus, it cannot satisfactorily shelter its King from Rook-checks.

ZUGZWANG *(n.)* A word from German that means "compulsion to move." In chess endgames it has a negative connotation. If a player is "in *Zugzwang*," any move he can make loses or worsens his position.

ZWISCHENZUG *(n.)* A German term meaning "intermediate move." Also called In-between Move. It's usually an unexpected move, such as a check, that allows a player to delay recapturing elsewhere for one move.

Index

About the Author

BRUCE PANDOLFINI is perhaps best known for his monthly *Chess Life* "ABC's of Chess" column and for his seven instructional chess books including *Bobby Fischer's Outrageous Chess Moves, Principles of the New Chess, Russian Chess, The ABC's of Chess, Let's Play Chess, Kasparov's Winning Chess Tactics,* and *One Move Chess by the Champions.* Perhaps the most experienced chess teacher in North America, and the executive director of the Manhattan Chess Club, Bruce Pandolfini lives in New York City.

Printed in the United States
By Bookmasters